PROFIT PATHOLOGY
AND OTHER INDECENCIES

PROFIT PATHOLOGY AND OTHER INDECENCIES

MICHAEL PARENTI

Paradigm Publishers
Boulder • London

All rights reserved. No part of the publication may be transmitted or reproduced in any media or form, including electronic, mechanical, photocopy, recording, or informational storage and retrieval systems, without the express written consent of the publisher.

Copyright © 2015 Paradigm Publishers

Published in the United States by Paradigm Publishers, 5589 Arapahoe Avenue, Boulder, CO 80303 USA.

Paradigm Publishers is the trade name of Birkenkamp & Company, LLC, Dean Birkenkamp, President and Publisher.

Library of Congress Cataloging-in-Publication Data

Parenti, Michael, 1933–
  Profit pathology and other indecencies / Michael Parenti.
    pages cm
  Includes bibliographical references and index.
  ISBN 978-1-61205-661-6 (hardcover : alk. paper)—
  ISBN 978-1-61205-829-0 (library ebook)—
  ISBN 978-1-61205-662-3 (pbk. : alk. paper)—
  ISBN 978-1-61205-830-6 (consumer ebook)
  1. Social classes—Political aspects—United States. 2. Power (Social sciences) 3. Wealth—Political aspects. 4. Capitalism—Moral and ethical aspects. 5. Equality. I. Title.
  HN90.S6P363 2015
  306.3'42—dc23
                                                                        2014042308
Printed and bound in the United States of America on acid-free paper that meets the standards of the American National Standard for Permanence of Paper for Printed Library Materials.

19 18 17 16 15   1 2 3 4 5

Contents

Part One: Class, Race, and Empire

Chapter 1 Thinking about the Great Class Divide   3

Chapter 2 Ethnicity and Exploitation: A Quick History of the Boiling Pot   11

Chapter 3 Empire in Extremis? Some Urgent Notations   25

Part Two: The Corporate Beast at Home

Chapter 4 A Case of Death and Profits   45

Chapter 5 Free Market Medicine: A Personal Account   57

Chapter 6 Free Market Medicine: More True Stories   67

Part Three: Cultural Aberrations and Other Oppressions

Chapter 7 Pedophiles, Popes, Priests, Preachers, and Papa   83

Chapter 8 Inequality: 85 Billionaires and the Poorer Half   101

Part Four: Global Rule and Ruin

Chapter 9 Capitalism, a Self-Devouring Beast   117

Chapter 10 Profit Pathology and Disposable Planet	133
Epilogue: The Next Trip	147
Notes	*151*
Index	*167*
About the Author	*175*

Part One

Class, Race, and Empire

1

Thinking about the Great Class Divide

WHEN WE LEAST EXPECT IT, when we slump disheartened not daring to hope for signs of popular uprising, seeing no movement on behalf of peace and social justice, there sometimes bursts forth a cry of resistance in one or more places. Unannounced, the anger of the common people so impressively shatters the deadening silence long imposed by the powers that be. Half the world wakes up. Suddenly the democracy takes to the streets. The ground itself seems to heave, as people ignite each other's spirits. And we dare to think that we might create some regenerative resurgence, that we might break through the repressive strictures and structures imposed by privileged powers.

An Awakening of Political Consciousness

No one predicted the Tunisian and Egyptian uprisings of January 2011, not the Middle East experts who serve in the US State Department and in the CIA, not the area specialists in academia, and certainly not the chatterbox media pundits who say so little about so much, followed by so much about so little. No one predicted the turmoil that surfaced in almost a dozen countries during the popular ferment that was labeled the Arab Spring. If they did expect these insurgencies, they very much kept it to themselves.

Likewise no one predicted the uprisings that were to boil over within the United States itself, beginning with Occupy Wall Street in September 2011, a protest movement that spread across seventy cities and hundreds of other US communities, followed immediately by similar Occupy actions in scores of other countries around the globe.

Among the impressive things about the Occupy movement was its explicit enunciation of *class conflict*. It did not begin as Occupy Capitol Hill or Occupy Pennsylvania Avenue or Occupy Fort Bragg. It skipped all the adjunct institutions and stalked the beast to its lair: It began as Occupy *Wall Street*. The target of protest was nothing less than the very heart of finance capital, the moneyed class whose wealth and power constrict our standard of living while having its way with our bedraggled republic and our battered environment.

With a daring plunge into reality, the Occupy movement in America issued pronouncements about the 1 percent who are exploiting the 99 percent, a perfect publicity formula, simple to use, yet saying so much, even occasionally winning the passing attention of some mainstream media commentators (if only to be scoffed at).

For decades some few of us have been urging others to focus on *the great class divide* that imposes its distorting and painful effect on life at home and abroad. Within the Occupy movement and without a moment's hesitation, people were now suddenly speaking about the

1 percent who grew obscenely rich off the backs of the 99 percent. Here was a long-awaited recognition of class exploitation in America.

The protestors carried signs uncovering the many disguises that class struggle assumes. Their posters and banners condemned the republic's terrible underemployment and the empire's endless wars, the environmental abuses and limitless profiteering perpetrated by giant corporations, and the enormous tax loopholes they enjoyed, the disheartening profit-driven abuses of our medical system, the immense inequality of incomes and cruel attrition of poverty, and the financial thievery perpetrated by banksters and other corporate gangsters who feed from the public trough. The Occupy movement put it all on the table, the very issues that the plutocratic interests would never care to address.

The Occupy movement was accorded very little respectful attention by the corporate media. Media people know for whom they work. Often do they gaze at the great class divide and see only harmony and goodwill. Often they dismiss the gross inequalities as a delusion fabricated by "conspiracy theorists" and other "self-appointed" agitators.

Over the last two decades or more, the professional opinion makers who overpopulate the Congress and the mainstream media have been denouncing as "class warfare" any criticism posted against the corporate rich. Popular protest against the mean but smooth system of financial expropriation is denounced as disruptive and divisive. If we listen to the powers that be, our society presumably enjoys a pastoral harmony among its various socioeconomic classes, save for some malcontents.

Class as a Dirty Word

Many members of the 1 percent will even insist that "class" is an archaic term that has no place in American political discourse. Yet they are the first to summon it up and point to themselves as victims of a *class war* supposedly launched by elements within the 99 percent. In other words, whenever we accuse them of perpetrating class war against *us*, they accuse us critics of instigating class war against *them*.

The very mention of the word "class" is a touchy matter in American political discourse. Class is a concept that is strenuously avoided by mainstream opinion makers, most economists and other academics, and even many who claim to be on the political left. When certain terms are eliminated from public discourse, so are certain thoughts. Dissident ideas become all the more difficult to pursue when there are no acceptable words to express them.

With the C-word out of the way as some kind of indecency, it is then easy to dispose of other politically unacceptable concepts such as class privilege, class exploitation, class interest, class power, and class struggle. These, too, are judged no longer relevant in a society that supposedly consists of the fluid pluralistic interplay of diverse "groups."

The moneyed class in this country has been pursuing class warfare against the working populace for more than two centuries. But when we point this out—when we marshal terms like *class warfare* and *class conflict* to describe the system of exploitation we live under—our indictments are dismissed as Marxist ranting, ever so indecent and divisive. And we are dismissed as ideologically inspired cranks. For decades, class has been dismissed as an outworn Marxist notion out of place in contemporary American society. It is a five-letter word that is treated like a dirty four-letter one.

Amanda Gilson put it perfectly: "The concept of 'class warfare' has been hi-jacked by the wrong class: the ruling class. The wealthy have been waging war silently and inconspicuously against the middle and the poor classes for decades! Now that the middle and poor classes have begun to fight back, it seems the rich want to try to call foul—the game was fine when they were the only ones playing it."[1]

The reactionary corporate rich have always denied that they themselves were involved in class warfare. Indeed, they insisted that no such thing existed in our harmonious prosperous society—if only the rest of us could understand that.

In the mainstream media, in political life, and in much of academia, "class" is still a verboten word. If you use it, you make your listeners uneasy ("Is the speaker a Marxist?"). In academia, one need only pose a question about the class interests involved in this or that issue and one is likely to be called out for pursuing doctrinaire Marxist notions. I speak from personal experience after working many years in academia.

There are costly sanctions if you persist in talking or writing about class exploitation and class inequity. Even more severe sanctions if you try to buttress your beliefs with *actions* on behalf of peace and social justice. You are likely not to get far in your journalism career or in public life or in academia, especially in fields like political science and economics. Again I can speak from the experiences of my career and the careers of others of kindred persuasion.

Most individuals involved in political discourse learn to talk *around* the subject of class conflict and class power. Instead of *working class*, we hear of "working families" or "blue collar" and "white collar employees." Instead of *lower class* we hear of "inner-city poor" and the "unemployed." Instead of the *corporate capitalist owning class*, we hear of the "more affluent" or the "upper quintile." Don't take my word for it, just listen to how the politicos speak. Many of them—like President Obama—settle for an even more cozy and muted term: *folks,* as in "Folks are strugglin' along," uttered in a folksy tone.

Class is used with impunity and mainstream approval only when it has that magic, neutralizing adjective "middle" attached to it. The *middle class* is an acceptable mainstream concept because it covers—rather than exposes—the great divide; it dilutes and muffles critical consciousness. A Pew survey in 2008 found that 91 percent of respondents believe they are either middle class, upper middle class, or lower middle class. Relatively few identify as working class. And most of the people who live in poverty are nevertheless reluctant to identify themselves as poor or lower class or even just working class.[2]

Americans have a most imperfect notion of how unequally wealth is distributed in their country. And they have little idea of how rich the super rich really are. Instead millions of us embrace the mythology that nearly everyone in America is middle class—except for a few fabulously rich and a minor stratum of very poor. Hence there is little room for any awareness of class conflict. That may be changing as the Great Recession of 2008 lingers on and on, bringing a sharp decline to the middle class and devastation to the previously more solvent elements of the working class.[3] The concept of middle class serves less well as a neutralizer when the middle class itself becomes a stark victim of capitalist rollback.

Class Power and Wealth

Class is also allowed to be used as a term of limited application when it is part of the holy trinity of *race, gender,* and *class*. Applied in that manner, the concept of class is reduced to a demographic trait related to lifestyle, consumption preferences, divorce rates, education levels, and income levels. In forty years of what was called *identity politics* and *culture wars,* class as a concept was diminished to something of secondary importance. All sorts of leftists and New Leftists told us how we needed to think anew, how we had to realize that class was not as important as race or gender or culture or ecology or personal liberation—as if class power did not have a crucial and bruising impact on all of these.

No, many of the New Leftists insisted, class does not occupy as important a role in life as these other demographic traits; it is a lesser component of identity politics. Race and gender are powerful and highly visible determinates of one's destiny, locked into one's very biology, and amplified by the prevailing racist/sexist culture—and many cultures around the world indeed harbor strong elements of racism and certainly sexism.

I was one of those who thought the concepts of race, gender, and class should not be treated as mutually exclusive of each other. In fact, they are interactive. Thus racism and sexism have always proved functional for class exploitation and oppression. Despite its omnipresent hold, class often has a lower visibility than race and gender—especially in the United States where we have been taught to be oblivious to the hidden injuries of class. Economic exploitation of us as workers, taxpayers, and consumers has been skillfully cloaked, especially in public discourse.

Some of us went further, pointing out that there is another definition of class that the propagators of identity politics have denied or at least overlooked, another reason to worry about the impact of class as a social force. Class should be seen as *a social relationship relating to wealth and power,* involving a conflict of material interests between those who own and those who work for those who own. Without benefit of reason or research, this latter usage of class is most definitely dismissed out of hand as Marxist. The narrow reductionist mainstream view of class as a demographic trait keeps us from seeing the extent of economic inequality and the severity of class power and class exploitation in society, allowing many researchers and political commentators to mistakenly assume that US society has no deep class divisions, no class conflicts of interest, and no problems of class power.

To repeat: We should think of class not primarily as a demographic trait but as a relationship to the means of production, as a relationship to power and wealth. Class is not an entity, it is a relationship: *class* as in slaveholder and slave, lord and serf, capitalist and worker; *class* as in class conflict, class exploitation, and class warfare.

Once we learn to talk about the realities of class power, we may be on our way to talking critically about *capitalism,* another usually verboten word in the public realm. And once we start a critical discourse about capitalism, we will be vastly better prepared to defend our own democratic and communal interests against capitalism's insatiable encroachments. Finally the 1 percent is finding it somewhat more difficult to manipulate the 99 percent. And perhaps the 99 percent are beginning to locate themselves within the context of class exploitation and class wealth. Perhaps they are beginning to think for themselves, an activity that is often strenuously frowned upon in a universe of discourse controlled by 1 percent or, as we shall see, even far less than 1 percent.[4]

2

Ethnicity and Exploitation
A Quick History of the Boiling Pot

From the early colonial period continuing into the late twentieth century, America was seen predominantly as an Anglo-Protestant preserve. For many Americans this was something of which to be proud. America also has been seen as a great Melting Pot, diverse peoples and cultures blended together to form a distinctly national amalgam. But the truth is less heartwarming than that. The process of multicultural amalgamation has been playing out within a context of social conflict, oppressive bigotry, and harsh economic exploitation—the kind of things seldom afforded serious consideration in this country's public discourse.

An American Holocaust

Celebrating the great Melting Pot makes it easier for us to overlook the unspeakable violence and brutality of the earliest ethnic encounters, specifically the holocaust waged against the indigenous Americans ("Indians"). Some early European settlements engaged in friendly exchanges with Native Americans. These contacts were beneficial mostly to the colonists who were untutored in the ways of wilderness survival. But instead of a melting or blending, this ethnic experience brought a firestorm of extermination—perpetrated by the land-grabbing, Bible-thumping white settlers otherwise hailed as "our forefathers."

In the centuries before Columbus, the indigenous peoples of what is now called North America lived well, husbanding their land without visiting ruination upon it. Their diets were wholesome, diverse, and well balanced, and they were given to hygienic practices. The Massachusetts Bay colonists attempted to "civilize and Christianize" native children by putting them in schools alongside their own white offspring. The native children, who wore relatively little clothing and bathed every day in lakes and rivers, could not stand the odors of the English children who rarely bathed and wore heavy clothing. More than once the native kids bolted out the schoolroom windows when they could no longer bear the stench.[1]

Worse still, the indigenous peoples had never been exposed to the toxic microbes carried by the white invaders. Hence, they had little opportunity to build up much physiological resistance. Mass portions of the native population were wiped out in plagues soon after contact with the European colonists.[2]

The lives of indigenous peoples in eastern North America—from quality of diet and medicine to individual freedom—were superior to the pinched, unwashed, dour lives transported from Christianized England. The Europeans were far more practiced than the Native Americans in dealing with syphilis, gonorrhea, small pox, typhoid, and bubonic plague, not to mention hangings, slavery, prostitution, religious wars, witch hunts, and inquisitions. European superiority registered in a few devilishly crucial areas, specifically the technologies of firearms, armor, and oceanic transport. The Native Americans had no desire to embrace the religiously oppressive, mean-spirited, acquisitive life of the colonizers. They lived comfortably free from any ruinous impulse for massive wealth accumulation. Labeled as "savage beasts" by the invaders, they actually behaved in courteous and kindly ways—that is, until they realized what they were up against.[3]

The indigenous peoples were subjected to heartless butcheries, beginning with the slaughter of the Arawak (Tainos) of Hispaniola in the 1490s. By the 1630s the Puritan settlers were launching attacks against the Pequot tribe, massacring hundreds of men, women, and children. The meager number of survivors were sold into slavery in the West Indies. In the 1680s, in the Chesapeake tidelands, there came another wave of mass killings. This was followed by two long centuries of merciless wars across the entire continent, ending with the treacherous slaughter of Lakota men, women, and children at Wounded Knee, South Dakota, in 1890.[4]

Estimates of the native population of America prior to the European conquest vary from 12 million to 18 million, composing more than six hundred distinct tribal societies, speaking over five hundred languages. But after four centuries of warfare, massacre, disease, and dispossession, the original population was reduced by over 90 percent, a holocaust whose magnitude remains largely unmatched and unrecognized today. Whole tribes were completely exterminated or whittled down to scattered numbers. In this way the "Wild West" was "tamed" and "settled." Today the Native American population has grown back to about 2.9 million, including Native Alaskan and Hawaiian peoples, and additional hundreds of thousands of people of mixed race origin, out of a total US population of some 310 million.[5]

Along with the destruction of Native Americans came the expropriation of native lands. "Speaking with forked tongue, the U.S.

government broke all of its 600-plus treaties and agreements with various indigenous nations," Brian Willson reminds us.[6] The native peoples were slaughtered with merciless deliberation and forethought so that their lands might be taken. The lands were not stolen as an afterthought. From the very beginning, the primary goal was not extermination but expropriation, not killing the natives per se, but grabbing the land and the fortune that comes with it: great and glorious expanses of farming lands and plains, mighty forests, green pastures and meadows with wild fruits, powerful rivers, wild herds and plentiful game, pristine waters, bays, lakes, fisheries, and inlets, beautiful hills and majestic mountains, deep ravines and vast deposits of rich minerals—all in unmatched abundance.

In quick order, the hostility felt toward the Native Americans took on a fury of its own. They were seen as "red devils," "wild dogs," "blood thirsty savages," and "heathens with souls consigned to hell." As the saying went: "The only good injun is a dead injun." So with most imperialist invasions, the victimized are depicted as victimizers. The heartless destruction of the native population was justified as an act of rectitude and self-defense against subhuman moral inferiors. Racism swiftly became the handmaiden of economic exploitation and imperialism.

Plundered Lands

So it was that America the Beautiful, God's gift to humanity, was conceived and long nourished in violent rapacity. The European colonists felt only fear and loathing for the "savages" who lurked about in the nearby woods. Hard-featured white men, hearts coldly brimming with Calvinist devotion, detested not only the savages but each other. As John Kozy remarks: "The totally impure Puritans of Massachusetts despised the Quakers of Pennsylvania and the Catholics of Maryland."[7]

Ethnicity and Exploitation: A Quick History of the Boiling Pot

The pitiless imperialists—beginning with Columbus and his accomplices—who discovered the "New World" were first impelled by the *auri sacra fames* (the cursed hunger for gold), followed by massive land seizures, natural resource acquisitions, and profitable slave labor. The lands were to be torn open and closed off, mined and mutilated; the forests hacked away; the soil overworked to erosion; the creeks blocked and buried; the fisheries depleted; and both the wild game and the inhabitants slaughtered to near extinction. The natural world was there to be plundered. The magic wilderness was to be transformed into a machine-fed garden, joylessly fenced acreage, with choice parcels allocated to the colonizers' leaders. To this day, the continent's living resources continue to be transformed into mass-market commodities, which, in turn, are transformed into dead capital. Living with nature gave way to accumulate, accumulate, accumulate, living against nature, ignoring the injuries done to the natural world.

In our day, the surviving Native American cultures have been greatly diminished for lack of a viable geopolitical base. Many Native Americans now live on reservations under conditions too severely narrowed to allow for a robust survival of indigenous ways. They may profess a revivalist dedication to their long-standing cultures, but in less ceremonial moments they wear blue jeans, speak English, drive pickup trucks, use power tools, watch television, attend school, and eat fast foods. In other words, while there has been relatively limited *assimilation* of Native Americans into the dominant Anglo-Protestant social structure, there has been a good deal of lifestyle *acculturation* imposed upon them by a mass-market society. Much the same can be said about other ethnic groups that subsequently came to these shores.

Meanwhile it must be kept in mind that today the Native Americans have long been deprived of their inheritance: the immeasurable natural wealth of a hugely rich continent. From sea to shining sea, it was taken from them—most often along with their lives.

Enslavement as Class Rule

The other ethno-class horror perpetrated within America's Boiling Pot was the African enslavement, another tale of misery that lasted centuries. A slave society is a class society in its rawest form of human exploitation. On the eve of the Civil War, approximately 3.2 million blacks lived in servitude (along with small numbers of white indentured servants). Theories supporting Caucasian superiority and black enslavement were promoted by academic teachings, "scientific" findings, and church sermons. Well into the twentieth century, Confederate apologists like Yale historian Ulrich Bonnell Phillips were turning out books depicting slaves as having been content and happily devoted to their kindly masters.[8]

The African chattels were deemed the *beneficiaries*, not the victims, of enslavement. They may have been forced to toil the entire day and much the night, but they also enjoyed exposure to an advanced society that far surpassed the backward ways of their less fortunate kin in "darkest Africa," or so it was argued. The very slaveholders who insisted that blacks were naturally incompetent took strenuous measures to keep them incapacitated. For instance, while claiming that chattels had no interest in literacy and no knack for it, the owners imposed the harshest interdictions against the ones who dared to learn how to read and write. In the planter's eye, slaves were not qualified to partake of civilized refinements that might inflate their aspirations or cause them to stake a willful course toward liberation.[9]

Over the years the slavers of various nations bought or kidnapped approximately 11.8 million Africans from their homelands, packing them into filthy hulls then carrying them across a vast ocean, the majority going to South America and the West Indies. An estimated one out of every five captives (more than 2 million) perished during this horrid transport known as the Middle Passage.[10] On the plantation, slaves who ran away from their overlords were hunted down with hounds and armed patrols. Recalcitrant captives were severely lashed, branded, chained, and in other ways tortured and degraded. Those who attempted rebellion were swiftly suppressed and usually hanged.[11] Whatever difficulties slaves might have caused, they still were greatly prized because of the services and rich returns their labor brought, including the agricultural, mining, mill, and timber goods they produced in such profitable amounts. Furthermore, slaves were both labor and capital. Beside the value their labor produced, they themselves were saleable and highly valued property.

Some slaves were allowed to develop skills that brought a profitable return or special service to the master. In George Washington's household, a slave named Hercules served as an expert chef and was treated well by the standards of that day. Nevertheless even he ran away, preferring an uncertain freedom to an endless subjugation.[12] Some slaves served as overseers. As in any imperialist system, selected individuals drawn from the chattel population were enlisted to help suppress their own people in return for meager rewards.

There were special horrors reserved for female slaves, who were subjected to rape and long-term concubinage by their masters. Drawing from his own years of bondage, Frederick Douglass describes a young black woman as one "who possessed that which is ever a curse to the slave-girl; namely—personal beauty."[13] In other instances, a female slave, deemed to be a healthy breeder, might be forced into marriage with a male slave not of her wanting, in what amounted to "an institutionalized form of rape commonly practiced on the plantation." [14] The goal was to produce numerous offspring who could be profitably worked or sold off.

An affluent and influential plantation master, possessed of much land and many slaves, lived as ruler of his own imperium, exercising a power of life and death over his chattels. As one historian concludes, "No more than a small fraction of Southern slaveholders felt even twinges of doubt and guilt" regarding slavery.[15]

A myth arose among some US historians that slavery was a costly and not really profitable form of labor. This notion is at variance with how the slaveholders themselves calculated things, they who lived off slave labor in lush opulence on grand plantations. What the slaves produced in value was many times more than what it cost to feed and house them.[16] People like James Madison came to this same calculation. As a slaveholder, shortly after the American Revolution, he told a visitor that he made $257 a year on every slave he owned and spent only $12 or $13 a year for a slave's keep. As early as 1820, American slaveholders owned 2 million slaves worth $1 billion, a third of all US wealth of that day, the biggest pool of collateral in the country.[17]

The Southern aristocracy profited enormously from slavery, as did the Northern elites. Slave trading was a highly profitable business for Yankee merchants. Just about every Northern city was involved in shipping and selling captives or marketing agricultural goods and other commodities produced by slave labor. Rhode Island—not Virginia or South Carolina—was the largest slave-trading state in the country.[18]

Slavery also advantaged the Ivy League schools and other elite colleges. At Yale and Harvard, elite sons often were from families involved in buying and selling people in bondage. The "scientific" ideas marshaled to justify slavery were contrived at Northern universities. Meanwhile, in the North as well as the South, abolitionist faculty members were removed from their teaching positions. "Ivy League schools were both early beneficiaries of the slave economy and 19th-century purveyors of racism in the guise of scholarship."[19] Enriched trustees and college presidents were linked to slave trafficking. Some of them, along with administrators, faculty, and students, had slave servants living at school. There also were slave crews that did the university's maintenance work.

For the Southern aristocrats, slavery was the bedrock of their class wealth. To maintain their beloved "peculiar institution," they were willing to plunge into a secessionist war that delivered four years of destruction and 620,000 American deaths. After the postwar period of Northern occupation known as Reconstruction (1865–1877), there came another century of slavery under a different name. Throughout the South more than 100,000 defenseless African Americans (or perhaps more than twice that number) were regularly arrested under the flimsiest charges, only to be sent to forced labor sites. County jail records show many thousands of African Americans being arrested while causing trouble to no one. They were charged with vagrancy, loitering, gambling, lack of personal identification, hitching freight trains, foul language, loud talking in public, talking to white women, and changing employers without permission.[20]

The conditions of control and punishment were much like those in antebellum times: forced labor without pay, and a servitude enforced with whips, chains, dogs, and guns. After serving their terms of peonage, captives were likely then to be slapped with additional trumped-up charges, unpaid fines, and the need to work off the inflated costs of their prison keep, which they invariably were unable to do. So they were incarcerated for endless periods. Some of their cruelest work was in the unsafe coal mines, where they perished in frightful numbers.

There was one crucial difference between antebellum slavery and this post-Reconstruction system of chain-gang incarceration. Slaves in earlier times were valued as property. They cost substantial sums and could be sold at a profit. But the convicts of the new postslavery system could be treated without the slightest care that one gives to property. "If they died while in custody, there was no financial penalty to the company leasing them."[21] They had no intrinsic market value. They could be done away with and easily replaced by other convicts at no cost.

Hundreds of forced labor camps sprang up across the South, operated by state and local governments and big corporations. The number of arrests varied not with crime waves but with the need for cheap labor. The rich investors who in the antebellum days used slaves to build railroads and toil on plantations and in coal mines, timber camps, and iron works were also the first to enslave black workers in the decades after Reconstruction.

Klan vigilante lynch mob rule further demoralized and terrified black communities. African Americans continued to be railroaded into chain gangs through much of the twentieth century, up at least until US entry into World War II (December 1941). It goes without saying that racial segregation and white supremacy contributed little to the much-vaunted Melting Pot. After generations of civil rights struggles, racism still festers in word and deed among civilians and police. One positive development: Few officeholders in the political mainstream feel free to talk openly like backwoods Klansmen. Facing charges of racial prejudice today, they usually are quick to issue denials in a manner not commonly witnessed in earlier eras.

African Americans and other minorities have attained positions in the professions, the judiciary, the military, the trade unions, the entertainment world, and other walks of life including politics. Yet the African American population remains disproportionately clustered at the bottom of the social pyramid, suffering ethno-class discrimination in many areas of life and work.[22] Racist attitudes continue to weave their way into everyday life, sometimes even in life-and-death situations such as that created by trigger-crazy police and biased courts and prisons. A black underclass helps to fill the prison cells and pad the profitable contracts of private prisons in a mass incarceration system. *There are more African Americans under correctional control today than were enslaved in 1850.*[23] Meanwhile, the enormous wealth extracted from forced black labor over the centuries remains without calculation or compensation.[24]

The Alien Hordes

Over the centuries, millions migrated to America in search of jobs and a better life. Much immigrant acculturation has been less a blending and more an obliteration of diverse cultures. One might agree with Peter Munch, a noted Norwegian American ethnologist, who suggests that the Melting Pot has been more like a "smelting furnace used to burn out the alien culture elements like slag from the pure metal of American culture."[25]

The earlier ethnic settlements were composed of European Protestants, 85 to 90 percent of whom were British (English, Scotch, Scotch-Irish, Welsh). Later came the Germans, Dutch, and Scandinavians. The real America, it was said, was not to be found in the swarthy, sweaty, polyglot, urban slums but in small-town, white Anglo-Saxon Protestant (WASP) America. Non-Protestants were treated with suspicion. In some states, into the early nineteenth century, Catholics and Jews were not allowed to vote or hold public office.

For almost 2,000 years, from Cicero to Jefferson, eminent leaders had warned their compatriots about the festering urban rabble, the lumpen scourge that eats away at a viable polity. Some of the immigrants did procure small parcels of land, even reconstructing rural communities that resembled those in the old country. But most immigrants were transformed into landless urban workers. As industry grew, so did the cities, for that was where the jobs were.

Well into the twentieth century the top leadership in professions and institutions continued to be predominantly WASP. In the big cities the ruling financial elites were Anglo-Protestant, for that was where the *big* money also happened to be. Consider the ethnic makeup of J.P. Morgan and Co. of New York. From 1895 to 1919 that investment firm had twenty-two men (no women, of course) who were partners. All were White Protestant; fourteen of them were Episcopalian and five were Presbyterian. All were of British antecedents and most were of upper-class upbringing. However, ethnic fissures can emerge even within the confines of class supremacy. Some Wall Street banking firms were run by Anglo-Protestants and others by Jews. WASP and Jewish bankers had numerous business dealings with each other, but they led separate social lives—given the in-group marriage preferences that prevailed among the Jews and the de rigueur anti-Semitism that prevailed among the WASP super rich.[26]

One great wave of immigrants, beginning in the 1840s, caused special alarm for Anglo-Protestant America. They were Northern European in origin, complexion, stature, facial appearance, and language. Yet they were not readily welcomed and were often the object of hateful discrimination: the Irish. By midcentury the Hibernians had arrived in such overwhelming numbers as to have an unsettling effect upon communities on the receiving end. The newcomers were utterly destitute, having been subjected in Ireland to the potato-crop famine and the brutal disregard manifested by British landlords. Worse than their pauperism was their popery; they were Roman Catholic at a time when Protestant America lived in fear and loathing of the Vatican's real and imagined reach.

Tight-faced Protestant preachers, well-born WASP reformers, and "Know-Nothing" nativists all sought to keep "the filthy Irish rabble" at bay, lest it infect American life with "rum, Romanism, and rebellion."[27] The Irish were seen as rambunctious, besotted, and lawless. Regardless of how unreceptive the Protestants might be, the Irish, a largely rural people, crowded into the urban cauldrons of America, destined to work at subsistence wages—when work was available—hired on the cheap by profiteering owners to toil as wage slaves in the mines, mills, railroads, and factories.[28]

The next great wave of immigration, 1870–1914, brought millions from Eastern and Southern Europe: Poles, Greeks, Jews, Italians, Russians, Portuguese, and others, the job-hungry hordes who spoke in strange tongues and worshipped the wrong god or, worse still, the right god in the wrong way. They, too, served the same purpose as the Irish before them, toiling long hours under severe conditions. In 1910 or thereabouts, scientist Henry Goddard applied intelligence tests to these newcomers and succeeded in convincing himself that almost 80 percent of every immigrant group was "feeble-minded."²⁹ Also among the presumably demented hordes thrown into the Boiling Pot were the various Asian peoples, who suffered unrewarding and often perilous labor conditions and who endured racial as well as class oppression.

Individual adventurers may seek far-off delights when they make passage abroad, but when whole populations of penniless people migrate, it is usually due to joyless politico-economic necessity. Preoccupied with ethnic differences, we tend to overlook our common class interests. Ethnic animosities—especially racism—have been used to play worker against worker, making them less willing to unite in common struggle against the owners and forcing them to compete for scarce community resources and meager wages.

Throughout history, rulers have played nationalities against each other. Aristotle, in his *Politics*, advised slaveholders to mix the nationalities of slave work gangs so that they might not easily concert against the master. Centuries later we find mining companies in America deliberately mixing Poles, Hungarians, Italians, and other nationals who usually spoke no English into the same work teams, thereby making them less able to form a common resistance.

Today the largest late-coming immigrant group are the Latinos, who actually have been migrating to North America for centuries but who now are arriving in larger-than-ever numbers, many as illegal immigrants. Their unlawful status makes them ever more reluctant to organize unions lest they be reported by their bosses to immigration officials for deportation.³⁰ At the same time, the revolutionary insurgencies of their compatriots in Central and South America have been subjected to brutal suppression by forces that are trained, equipped, and financed by the US national security state.³¹

A metaphoric image of ethnicity in the United States other than the Melting Pot (and the Boiling Pot) is the Quilt or the Mosaic. We are told that America is a Great Mosaic of diverse groups all living side by side. This image is almost as misleading as the Melting Pot.

Our mix of ethnic groupings does not constitute a mosaic but a parceled hierarchy. The groups are socially ranked by ethnicity and class. Even in early New England, Anglo-Protestant patrician families like the Endicotts, Winthrops, Bradfords, Lowells, and Cabots were not only at the top of the ethnic pile but at the apex of the class structure: "Where the Lowells talk only to the Cabots; and the Cabots talk only to God." Meanwhile there are Anglo-Protestants who arrived in America in the early or late migrations whose descendants to this day remain poor enough to be nastily labeled "white trash" or "trailer trash."

The point of all this discussion about ethnic conflict and violence is not to show how miserably divisive human beings can be—although that certainly should give us pause—but to argue that hostility between groups is not just the result of homegrown prejudices. Ethnic conflict is a component of the pursuit of wealth and the struggle to exploit labor and win supremacy over the land with all its riches. The goal is to live well at the expense of others.

More often than not, the divisions of belief, language, religion, and race blur the attempts to unify along class lines. The diverse groups divide against each other rather than uniting against the powerful few, the 1 percent who—no matter how removed they may be—are likely to be the major source of their tribulation.

3

Empire in Extremis?
Some Urgent Notations

THROUGH MUCH OF HISTORY the abnormal has been the norm. This is a paradox to which we should attend. It is true even of American history, contrary to what we have been taught in school. Our history has been filled with imperial aggrandizements and atrocities, so plentiful as to form a terrible normality of their own.

A Terrible Normality

The number of innocents massacred throughout world history are more than we can record. In the previous chapter, we noted the extermination of many *millions* of indigenous peoples throughout North America, extending over four centuries or more, continuing into recent times down into the Amazon region. There were the centuries of heartless slavery in the Americas and elsewhere, followed by a full century of lynch mob rule and Jim Crow segregation in the United States, and today the numerous killings and unwarranted incarcerations of black males by law enforcement agencies.

Let us mention the extermination of some 200,000 souls in the Philippines by the US military at the beginning of the twentieth century, the genocidal massacre of 1.5 million Armenians by the Turks in 1915, and the mass killings of African peoples by the Western colonizers, including the 63,000 Herero victims in German Southwest Africa in 1904, and the brutalization and enslavement of millions in the Belgian Congo from the late 1880s until emancipation in 1960—followed by years of neocolonial free market exploitation and repression in what was Mobutu's Zaire. French colonizers killed some 150,000 Algerians. Later on, several million souls perished in Angola and Mozambique at the hands of the Portuguese imperialists. Then there was an estimated 5 million in the merciless region now known as the Democratic Republic of the Congo.[1]

The twentieth century gave us—among other horrors—more than 16 million lost and 20 million wounded or mutilated in World War I, followed by the estimated 62 to 78 million killed in World War II, including some 24 million Soviet military personnel and civilians, 5.8 million European Jews, and taken together, several million Serbs, Poles, Roma, and other nationalities, in addition to thousands of homosexuals.

In the decades after World War II, many, if not most, massacres and wars have been openly or covertly sponsored by the US national security state. This includes the 2 million or so Vietnamese left dead or missing, along with 650,000 Cambodians, 100,000 Laotians, and 58,000 Americans. In recent years in much of Africa, Central Asia, and the Middle East there have been smaller wars, replete with atrocities of all sorts. Colombia, Guatemala, Honduras, El Salvador, and other places too numerous to list suffered the massacres and death squad exterminations of hundreds of thousands at the hands of US counterinsurgency forces. In Mexico a "war on drugs" has taken 70,000 lives with 8,000 missing. There was the slaughter of more than half a million socialistic or democratic nationalist Indonesians by the US-supported Indonesian military in 1965, eventually followed by the extermination of 100,000 East Timorese by that same US-backed military.

Consider the seventy-eight days of NATO's aerial destruction of Yugoslavia, especially Serbia, complete with depleted uranium, and the US bombings and/or invasions of Panama, Grenada, Somalia, Libya, Syria, Yemen, Western Pakistan, and Afghanistan. And as of 2014, the US-sponsored sanctions against Iran are seeding severe hardship for the civilian population of that country. Then there is the destruction done to the Iraqis on a grand scale by Washington's repeated bombings and invasion of their lands.[2] At the same time, thousands have died or been wounded in Israel's continuing war against Palestine. And Ukrainian reactionaries have been killing abundant numbers of Russian-speaking rebels and civilians in eastern Ukraine.[3]

A truly comprehensive inventory of deaths in imperial wars would fill volumes. And then there are the many millions who survive wars and massacres but remain forever broken in spirit with a lifetime of grieving, suffering, and pitiless privation. Think also of the millions of women and children around the world and across the centuries who have been trafficked in unspeakable ways, and the millions upon millions trapped in exploitative toil, be they trafficked slaves or indentured servants and laborers. Add to that the countless acts of repression, incarceration, torture, and other criminal abuses that beat upon the human spirit throughout the world day by day. In almost all these instances, empire and wealth have been the moving force.

Violence as the Ultimate Authority

We must not ascribe these aberrations to happenstance, innocent confusion, and unintended consequences. Nor, in regard to US foreign policy, should we believe the usual rationales about spreading democracy, fighting terrorism, providing humanitarian rescue, protecting our national interests, and other such scenarios. All this destruction and slaughter has greatly profited those plutocrats who pursue acquisition of natural resources, expansion of markets, cheap labor, and capital accumulation.

Ruling interests are well served by their superiority in firepower and striking force. Violence is what we are talking about here, not the wild and impulsive type but the persistent and well-organized kind, often conducted by the military or the secret agencies of state. Large-scale violence is the instrument of ultimate authority. Violence allows for the conquest of entire lands and the riches they contain. With a strong advantage in violence, the imperialists are able to exploit or exterminate multitudes while expropriating the fruits of their land and labor. These occurrences must be seen as something more than just abnormalities driven by happenstance or human depravity.

Resource Acquisition

What motivates the creation and expansion of empires? The dominant socioeconomic system reaching across the world today is free market capitalism in all its variations. Who benefits and who pays? The real story is at variance with the one we are usually fed by pundits and policy makers. The great imperative behind the imperial drive for expansion is the accumulation of value or, if you prefer, the acquisition of wealth, which is a different way of saying the same thing.[4]

Capital accumulation abroad often is an extraterritorial rendition of capital accumulation at home. Whether the copper mines are in

Montana or in Chile, the investors strive for ownership of the mineral resources, brushing aside the land claims of indigenous inhabitants. At the same time, the investors strive mightily to foist upon the host country or state (be it Chile, the United States, or the state of Montana) some of the costs of production, including the infrastructure of roads, bridges, harbors, and disposal of waste products. When necessary, the big companies have used well-bribed lawmakers, corrupt constables, and murderous gun thugs to break the resistance of local populations. From Colombia to the Philippines to Nigeria, government agents, gendarmerie, and courts force indigenous peoples to move from resource-rich homelands onto missionary reservations or vast shanty towns, so to live in acute desolation, their precious lands stolen from them forever.

Cheap Labor and Outsourcing

Digging mines in Montana, Chile, or anywhere else is an inviting financial venture for the corporations involved only if there is a sufficient pool of relatively disadvantaged workers living in the area or easily transported to it. By "disadvantaged" I mean workers who have nothing to sell but their labor power and who, greatly outnumbering the jobs available, must settle for whatever they can get. They are compelled to toil under wretched and often risky conditions for the barest recompense. Sometimes deprived of their meager wages, they end up in conditions akin to servitude. Slavery often has been the solution to the need for a cheap and available labor supply. Today, millions of people are still trafficked as work slaves or sex slaves in almost every part of the world including Europe and the United States.[5]

Transnational corporations might descend upon lands that have little resource wealth but much cheap labor. Instead of paying workers in Ohio $25 an hour plus benefits, an American company might move to a lower wage market in Alabama. And when workers in Alabama begin to organize for better wages, the company packs up and settles in Mexico and then eventually off to Indonesia, Bangladesh, Haiti, Nigeria, or some other country with a highly exploitative politico-economic order, so suppressive that many workers are obliged to toil for twelve cents an hour.

A company like Nike goes through the expense of outsourcing its entire production system, exporting even its machinery and technical materials to Indonesia because wages are so low in that country and value-added profit margins are so big. The Nike shoes are not then sold for a strikingly lower price back in the United States. They still cost us at least as much as when made in the US. Nike does not go all the way to Indonesia in order to help American consumers save money. The imperial investor enjoys a monopoly advantage at the production end and again at the selling end. Nike outsources in order to reduce labor costs substantially while maintaining high prices when selling in the United States and elsewhere, thereby vastly increasing profits.[6]

Mistreating the Environment

Mining companies do not venture into Montana, Chile, West Virginia, Bolivia, Canada, the Congo, or wherever in order to advance the quality of life for the local populations. Nor do they preserve the environment's precious viability when cutting down rain forests, removing mountaintops, drilling for oil, or fracking for gas. The natural environment is treated both as a limitless resource and a global trash can. Abundant communal lands are turned into toxic wastelands. Such irresponsible plunder minimizes production costs and maximizes profits, as the firm's diseconomies are foisted upon both the commonweal and the Earth's ecology. Corporations get rich by mistreating the environment.

Underdevelopment and Overexploitation

Some centuries ago, most of the Third World was not desperately impoverished and depleted. People lived modestly to be sure but often amid an abundance of game, fresh water, and plant foods that could be gathered or readily propagated. By now, however, many areas of the world have been ravaged. Unless corporate investors are outsourcing in a cheap labor market, they do not usually go into poor locations to enrich themselves. They go into *rich* areas—that is, rich in resources. By the time they are done, the region is likely to be sadly disfigured, stripped of whatever offerings it once had. Indigenous populations become indigent populations. Previously self-sufficient, they are reduced to penury, driven from the land and piled into the rotting shanty towns of teeming metropolises.

Much of the world's population is poor today not because people suffer from underdevelopment but from *overexploitation*. Walter Rodney, a prominent Guyanese scholar and political activist, who was assassinated in 1980 for telling too much truth, had it right when he titled a book he wrote *How Europe Underdeveloped Africa*. Rodney used "underdeveloped" as a verb rather than an adjective. The grinding poverty of underdevelopment was not an original historical condition, Rodney is saying. Underdevelopment is something that Europe has inflicted upon Africa, an overexploitation that has left so much of the continent impoverished while producing great riches for the plundering investors.[7] To call a poor Third World country a "developing nation" is to assume that it is belatedly emerging from a retarded stage; in fact, it is struggling against a colonial rapacity that has left it pitifully overexploited. The Western investors take out vastly more capital from a Third World country than they ever put in, thereby extracting wealth for themselves and creating poverty for others, a poverty they then call "underdevelopment." These Third World "developing nations" are usually doing relatively little developing. If anything, their people are sinking deeper into poverty.

Monopoly Control

Empires always strive for monopoly control. In earlier times such control was achieved by direct colonization. There was no need for British investors to share India's resources and markets with other nations. India, after all, *belonged* to the British empire—and the empire's plutocracy set the conditions for investment and production. So the colonizers grew richer while the Indian population grew poorer. From 1850 to 1900, India's per capita income dropped by almost two-thirds. Beginning in the early nineteenth century, Indian textile goods were driven off the market and textile centers like Dacca and Madras were forcefully shut down by the British colonialists who then flooded Indian markets with British textiles manufactured in Manchester. The Indians were left to raise the cotton and other raw materials. Such has been the fate of much of the Third World after years of imperial rule.[8]

Paying the Costs of Empire

The colonizers did not pay the costs of colonialism. They imposed all sorts of taxes and duties upon subdued populations so that the latter paid for their own oppression. Failure to comply often led (and still leads) to incarcerations, forced evacuations, massacres, and famines. Under the rule of foreign colonizers or corporate investors, the indigenous peoples are compelled to work at near starvation wages. So the colonizer not only steals the people's land but also their labor power. The costs of imperialism can be measured not just in material losses but in the horrifying loss of lives and loss of human happiness.[9]

Empires are costly undertakings. Navies, armies, and gendarmerie have to be financed. Overseas leaders and officials have to be paid off. As just noted, much of the money to pay for imperialism is extracted from the colonized population, but the rest is borne by the imperium's own people. The American public repeatedly supports US military interventions abroad, convinced that the enormous sums are for defending America, not for serving the corporate global empire.

Every year over a trillion dollars of the federal budget is allocated for military forces, bases, armaments, wars, and other imperial costs, reassuringly designated as defense spending, compliments of US taxpayers. Meanwhile federal, state, and local governments sink deeper into debt, face budget crises, cut back on human services, and close schools, hospitals, and libraries, while leaving roads, bridges, and other infrastructure unrepaired. Social needs are neglected so that the empire may excel in its global ventures. The empire feeds off the republic.

Not Too Costly for the 1 Percent

It has been noted that empires sometimes cost more than they are worth. The gains that are made by rich transnational corporations—through resource plunder, cheap labor, debt, and captive markets—are less than the costs of military bases, wars, foreign aid, and bribes. So the British spent far more on India than they took out of India—and they took out quite a bit. Likewise with the Americans in their control of the Philippines or their presence in Central America and the Middle East. Scholars like Timothy Parsons argue that while past empires produced an extractive surplus that exceeded the costs of conquest and governance, today the costs of conquest and governance exceed gains. The United States has spent several trillion dollars on Iraq and Afghanistan and nothing to show for it except enormous additional debts. From this, Parsons and others conclude that the policy is misdirected and irrational.[10]

But while these ventures may be irrational for society as a whole, they are not irrational for the businesses that profit from them without paying their costs. The wars brought tremendous profits to private security firms like Blackwater and scores of other contractors, including the military supply industry, and for whoever ripped off the hundreds of billions that the Pentagon says it cannot account for. To repeat: Those who pay the costs of empire are not the same as those who enjoy the gains. It is the 1 percent who accumulate the wealth of empire and the 99 percent who pay the taxes and suffer deterioration in their own domestic services and standard of living.

Let us say the United States spends $6 billion a year to protect a $3 billion investment in the Philippines; one might hastily conclude that empire is not a winning proposition. But in fact we in the 99 percent pay out the $6 billion and those in the 1 percent own the $3 billion in investments. Without hesitation those at the top of the pyramid will spend $2 of your money to protect $1 of theirs. In fact, when it comes to protecting their money, your money is no object. So when discussing imperialism, the prime unit of analysis usually should be the *economic class* rather than the nation-state. But these realities are seldom brought up in mainstream discourse.

An Empire in Decline?

Today one hears that the US empire is in decline. In fact, it has never done better, with military bases in more countries than ever—over 150 nations. Many of these bases are larger and more elaborately equipped than ever, with a newly ferocious and mobile striking power.

Along with direct military attacks against smaller countries, the US empire has employed techniques of nation-state destabilization and subversion (often called regime change). The US empire has effected regime changes across the globe, pouring billions of dollars into troubled countries to transform them into more compliant satellite states. Hundreds of nongovernment organizations (NGOs) join the disruptive fray, providing well-trained and well-financed "democratic protesters" equipped with color-coordinated banners, flags, and T-shirts, along with food supplies, tents, and portable toilets, and vast numbers of leaflets and posters in various languages. These things are accompanied by media crews and news reports circulated throughout the world with favorable treatment going to the regime changers. In addition, cadres trained in inciting disruption, sometimes equipped with firearms and Molotov cocktails, make hit-and-run appearances. Other mercenaries and "specialists" are called upon to provide secret death squads, snipers, and other assassins. Many countries also have police and paramilitary and military units that are trained, equipped, and financed by the United States to be used in forcing a definitive regime change.[11]

Unlike most true protestors, these attackers operate with the most powerful imperialist forces at their backs, giving them a persistent audacity that the besieged governments are seldom able to sustain. They storm the barricades and government buildings and disrupt parliamentary proceedings, as in the Serbian coup of 2000, the Georgian coup of 2003, the Ukrainian coup of 2014, and coups in Croatia and Kosovo, along with earlier regime changes throughout much of Eastern Europe. In addition, there has been the destabilizing riots and assassinations in Venezuela and Ukraine, along with the bloody bombings, military coups, and invasions in Guatemala, El Salvador, Nicaragua, Chile, Honduras, Panama, Iraq, Afghanistan, Grenada, Yugoslavia, Thailand, and numerous other countries, all financed and sponsored largely by the US national security state.[12] So the imperium's global warriors have shown unswerving vim and violence in smashing countries and movements that dared to stake out economically independent and reformist courses.

Given the global plutocracy's repeated successes, why think the empire is in decline? Perhaps because, as noted earlier, the empire feeds off the republic—and it is the *republic* that is much in decline, not the

1 percent. The imperium's ventures are immensely profitable for the wealthy few but they are a terrible burden for ordinary citizens who pick up the costs of imperialism, and a terrible cost to masses of people around the world whom the empire targets.

From Imperialism to Neo-Imperialism

At some point in history, the aggrandizers move from naked imperialism to neo-imperialism or, to put it another way, from colonialism to neocolonialism. When faced with resistance from the colonized populace, the imperialists eventually move to a less visible mode of superordination. The colonized country is granted the trappings of independence: its own flag, constitution, anthem, army, currency, and state leaders. In turn, the transnational corporations retain de facto control of the country's natural resources and refineries, land and agriculture, mines and mills, much of its labor and wage scales, and most of its imports, exports, finances, and markets.

Latin America provides dramatic examples of long-standing colonial rule overthrown by revolutionary struggle only to be transformed into neocolonial rule. Most Latin American countries were colonies of the Spanish crown from the early 1500s to the early 1800s. After finally achieving independence, they soon felt the economic and political muscle of the "Colossus of the North," whose overseas ventures are directed largely by financial and manufacturing interests hungry for natural resources, markets, and cheap labor buttressed by repeated occasions of direct military intervention.

Not Power for Power's Sake

The rise of neo-imperialism should tell us what imperialism is about: not glory and dominion, although those themes might be trumped up now and then. The imperial power seeks dominance so that the moneyed interests in one country can defeat other leaders and other nations so better to pursue their own interests. The aggrandizers are not seeking glory but control of natural resources, markets, labor forces, and profitable investment opportunities.

Truth be told, Colonel Blimp was in India not just to lord over the Indians with swagger stick in hand but also to make India a highly profitable place for the British royalty and plutocracy.

Not Racism for Racism's Sake

Imperialists do not pursue conquests against people of other races simply out of mean-spirited impulse. Western Europe's first colonial victims were in Eastern Europe; they were Caucasians just like the people in Western Europe. England's oldest standing colony was another white country: Ireland. The US imperial wars against Yugoslavia, Iraq, Libya, Syria, and several other countries involved large white populations along with some smaller groups of more varied hues.

While racism is not a motivating concern for the colonialists, it soon becomes a useful excuse. When the imperialists destroy the farms, mills, mines, and communities of indigenous peoples for purposes of gainful expropriation, racist excuses become handy justifications—as we have seen in the previous chapter regarding Native Americans. When you slaughter a people and steal their land and burn their townships and crops, you have to start thinking of them as less than human, as capable of the cruelest and most vicious atrocities. The victims, not the victimizers, are readily characterized as murderous devils with no souls. So today Washington keeps weaker countries in line with "humanitarian" bombings. The American public, usually reluctant to commit American troops to yet another military conflict, are once again swept along, convinced that the next bloodletting is necessary and noble in its goals.

Real Moderation

Along with opposing the crimes of corporate capitalism and the imperial state, we need to ask *why* such iniquities exist. What interests perpetrate the cruelties we witness? *Cui bono?* Who benefits?

During these struggles, many critics have taken care to genuflect obediently before the altar of anticommunism. They never talked critically about capitalism without also casting a stone at past or present communist countries, thereby showing how their ideology was "nuanced" and never too one-sided. Some of them still carry on in this manner. Not being one of them, I was repeatedly labeled an extremist not only by those who were much further to the right on the political spectrum but also by some of those on the left, the balancers whom I just described. But I persist in calling myself a *moderate*. This claim probably has never been taken seriously by ideological critics, but it is genuinely proffered. As I have explained in many public talks, there is nothing extreme about wanting people to have decent housing and employment, good schools and safe neighborhoods, while enjoying a social order that is free of racism, sexism, and other hatreds. What is so extreme about wanting to end class exploitation and the obscene accumulations and privileges of the super rich? Is it extreme to want massive cuts in a military budget that is vitiating our national capacity to provide decent human services? What is so extremist about wanting to save the environment while opposing destructive, murderous wars against nations that strive for peaceful self-development? No, we are not extremists. The extremists are already in power.

The American interventionists rely on the ultimate authority of force and violence. To maintain a superiority of force in the world, a superiority of firepower, mobility, and communications—an unmatched technology of destruction and domination—is to wield a strong hand over world policies. Not security but supremacy is the reason why US leaders find it necessary to build hundreds of bases around the world. But the cost is staggering, reducing the republic to dire debt.

During the Obama era we have witnessed an expansion of military operations, both covert and overt, directed at countries and political movements that seek to use their human and material resources for self-development. China and Russia are characterized as dangerous competitors of the United States to be isolated and outdone. Governments in Africa, Central Asia, Eastern Europe, and Latin America that try to go their own way are undermined and reduced to neoliberal satellite regimes that adhere to US global policies. Extremism at work.

Soft Imperialism

Soft imperialism—or what erstwhile secretary of state Hillary Clinton called "soft power"—includes capturing the targeted country's lifestyles and tastes, stoking a consumer mentality that includes fast cars and fast foods, rock concerts and superstars. Meanwhile the global airwaves are flooded with news media of a kind that echo US and other Western news media.

Religion also is a handmaiden of soft—and not so soft— imperialism, as religion has long been. Centuries ago, during the invasions of Central and South America, the conquistadors brought their priests to help subdue the Aztec and Mayan peoples. Centuries later, all through Latin America, Africa, and elsewhere, the church spread the gospel of obedience and devotion to the powers that be. Today fundamentalist Protestant missionaries in Central America explain to battered populations that their misfortunes have been brought upon themselves because they sided with wicked communist rebels and opposed the US-backed military governments, resulting in their being slaughtered in great numbers by the military and by US-supported death squads.[13]

All sorts of religious cults, from Bible-thumping evangelicals to saffron-robed Hare Krishnas, were sent into Russia in the early 1990s to help undermine economic collectivism and replace it with interior migrations of the soul. Washington also became a great supporter of Tibetan Buddhism, especially of that particular denomination financed partly by the CIA and dedicated to fomenting internal unrest within Tibet.[14] In some countries US-sponsored evangelical schools cooperate with the oil interests to crowd out the indigenous people. Secular educational programs and textbooks are also rewritten to promote the idea that Western imperialism does not exist and that all outside investment is beneficial for the indigenous population.

Educating collaborationist leaders to take over the reins of government when regime change is activated is another long-standing practice of soft imperialism. Special programs are set up to train the political and military leadership. Many leaders in Mexico, Iraq, Afghanistan, Libya, and Yugoslavia had put in time at Harvard or other prestigious US institutions before taking the reins of power.

Asking Why

We have to learn to ask why. Why do US leaders show inconsistency in supporting some terrible rulers and opposing other terrible ones? In fact, US policy is impressively consistent in its goals, albeit varied in its methods. Whether the recipient of US aid is a dictator or an elected leader, a practitioner of democratic rule or a torturer (or both), is not of central concern. The leaders of countries who are targeted for US destabilizing actions, sanctions, or military attacks and invasions can be democratically elected or autocratic. The CIA has openly admitted it uses torture.[15] The agency is known to have overthrown democratically elected leaders such as Allende in Chile, Aristide in Haiti, Milosevic in Yugoslavia, and dozens of others. The US has also attacked autocrats who commit economic nationalism, who refuse to fall into step and become satellites of US policy, such as Saddam Hussein in Iraq and Muammar Qaddafi in Libya.

What is constant in these scenarios is the presence of giant corporate cartels and their tireless pursuit of wealth. Above all they must work tirelessly to make the world safe for the Fortune 500, that is, the giant transnational corporations that own so much of the world.

The US empire is not in decline but it is under siege in a number of places. Like all empires, it lives by the sword, using deception and destruction. It lives to plunder and accumulate. It uses imaginary enemies to frighten its own people, but it also incites real enemies who loathe its retrograde ways. For democracy and our own salvation, for equality and environment, for peace and social justice, we must oppose the empire. And we can best do that when we know what it is really about, when we move from a liberal complaint to a radical analysis. Only then can we capture the heart of the matter.

Part Two

The Corporate Beast at Home

4

A Case of Death and Profits

WITHIN A RELATIVELY SMALL COMPONENT of a large politico-economic system, we sometimes can find a replica of the entire system itself. To understand the totality, it is sometimes worth closely investigating the particularity. (The ontogeny recapitulates the phylogeny.) In this chapter we will look at a particular kind of corporation, a privately owned power utility, and we will see how it reflects, in its way, the profiteering, deceptive practices, and criminal irresponsibility of the entire corporate system itself.

For generations the American public has been subjected to an ideological bombardment, financed by moneyed interests and directed toward glorifying private corporate success—while casting dark shadows of distrust upon nonprofit and public ownership. We are taught to believe that private, for-profit enterprises are more efficient, more trustworthy, and less expensive than publicly owned ones. Let us dwell on that for a brief spell. Here we consider the case of one of the nation's largest private utilities.

A Private Profiteering Utility

Pacific Gas and Electric (PG&E) is a multibillion-dollar privately owned, publicly regulated utility that enjoys a captive market of 15 million customers in northern and central California. As a corporate enterprise its prime function is to make enormous profits for its shareholders at whatever the cost to ratepayers and taxpayers. I know this from experience; I am one of California's taxpayers and one of PG&E's ratepayers.

The California Public Utilities Commission (PUC), the state regulatory agency, permits PG&E to increase rates that are *30 percent higher than the national average.* Meanwhile PG&E's shareholders enjoy a steady, above-average yearly return on equity. The utility is a shining monument to state-supported, monopoly capitalism. If costs rise, then so do customer rates (in order to guarantee favorable returns for shareholders). PG&E carries a $17 million insurance premium and additional millions in insurance deductibles; these expenses, too, are picked up by us, the ratepayers.

If northern and central California's gas and electric services were *publicly owned,* then the utility would be the public's property; it would be owned by the taxpayers and residents and would be run on a nonprofit basis. That means, its enormous earnings would not go into the pockets of private investors but would go into the public state budget and put to use for public needs—to the benefit of taxpayers and other residents. A system that uses this type of publicly owned, not-for-profit company for economic activities tightly related to the public good is called *socialism*. There would be no large skim off the top going to rich investors, no outrageously fat salaries, bonuses, and huge severance packages ("golden parachutes") pocketed by top executives, no billions of dollars in private wealth to be traded on the stock exchange. Customer rates would be almost one-third lower than they are today. And, even more important, gas pipelines would very likely be in better repair.

A Disaster with More to Follow

Let us dwell on that last point. Along with all the other expenses they bear, PG&E's ratepayers pay for the enormous costs of utility accidents. Consider the mortal terror visited upon San Bruno, California, in September 2010. A PG&E pipeline blew apart, producing a giant fireball that ripped through the San Bruno community, taking the lives of eight people, injuring over fifty others (some very seriously), and completely destroying or seriously damaging more than a hundred homes. An official from the National Transportation Safety Board described it: "My immediate assessment was the amazing destruction, the charred trees, the melted and charred cars, the houses disappeared."[1]

In the weeks before the catastrophe, residents had been reporting gas odors and had voiced fears about an ongoing leak and an impending disaster waiting to happen. These complaints brought no action from the company. A state assemblyman from the San Bruno area noted that the torn pipeline was over sixty years old, having been installed in 1948. He criticized PG&E for its poor maintenance and lax response. After the explosion, it took the company almost three hours to shut off the gas emission.

Company officials had known since 2007 that the aged pipeline serving San Bruno needed to be replaced. As reported by The Utility Reform Network (TURN), a public interest group, the PUC had granted PG&E a $5 million rate increase to replace the pipeline in 2009, but the company never got around to doing the work. Instead PG&E overspent its budget on executive bonuses while delaying pipeline replacement for another four or five years, in what amounted to criminal negligence.[2] But nobody went to jail.

Then the utility had the gall to request yet another $5 million rate increase to cover the cost of replacing the very same section of pipeline that it had neglected for so long. The disastrous September 2010 explosion likely would have been averted if the utility had dealt with the pipeline several years earlier as originally slated.

Further investigation revealed that PG&E was guilty of faulty and suspiciously erroneous record-keeping in the documents filed with the PUC. The utility apparently tried to conceal this problem. It was aware of the serious flaws in its records but failed to report them for almost a year. Faulty records, cover-ups, and maintenance negligence and blunders were deemed to be among the key causes of the San Bruno tragedy.[3] TURN, the consumer group, was calling for $13.1 million in fines against PG&E for breaking the rules and covering up its wrongdoing.

Over a year later, federal investigators issued a blistering report denouncing PG&E for "a litany of failures" that led to the deadly San Bruno blast. The feds from the National Transportation Safety Board accused the company of ignoring over the years clearly visible warnings that could have prevented the disaster. They faulted PG&E for its poor record-keeping, its inadequate pipeline inspection practices, and its long delay in shutting off the gas feeding the conflagration, a blast that incinerated an entire neighborhood and took so many victims.[4]

PG&E has a history of dangerous mishaps: Improper piping allowed gas to leak from a mechanical coupling in 2006, and a leak in Rancho Cordova led to an explosion that killed one resident and injured two others in 2008. There have been more than forty other accidents in just the past decade. These included power outages, gas leaks, natural gas fires, pipeline explosions (some of which involved additional fatalities), and electrocution of employees.[5]

One can only wonder how many California communities are still at risk from an aging and deficient utility infrastructure. Quite a few—if we believe the Consumer Protection and Safety Division of the California PUC. In 2012 it reported that over the past forty years, PG&E had put its customers in jeopardy by failing to reduce pressure on 898 sections of gas pipelines. These lines were being run at pressures considered unsafe for populated areas or were inspected too infrequently, said the state regulators.[6]

Let the Public Pay

PG&E did not dispute its own culpability—as far as words go. But more than two years after the explosion in San Bruno, company spokespersons still insisted that ratepayers should pay about 90 percent of the proposed $2.2 billion in improvements to the gas transmission system. As the *Contra Costa Times* commented, PG&E has wanted its customers "to pay almost the entire cost to remedy the utility's incompetence in getting the job done right the first time," even though "the utility has the financial wherewithal to pay for most if not all of the $2.2 billion in bringing its pipeline system up to decent safety standards without significantly increasing rates."[7]

PG&E's attempt to be exempted from punitive damages in lawsuits filed by more than 350 people in connection with the San Bruno disaster was rejected in court. Settlements were deemed obligatory. In April 2014, PG&E was indicted on twelve criminal charges and now faces $6 million in fines and other charges relating to San Bruno.

Still it was not likely that any corporate moguls would end up in prison. The Public Utilities Commission, like most state and federal regulatory agencies, is never too harsh or rigorous with the industry it is supposed to be regulating. In July 2014, a top PUC staff person was caught advising a top PG&E executive on how to deflect requests for public information that might prove embarrassing to the utility. The state commission seemed to be acting more as a consultant for PG&E than as a regulator who defends the public interest.[8]

PUC was considering a penalty of $2 billion for alleged safety lapses, with nothing said about criminal law actions against the utility. PG&E claimed that it had paid approximately $565 million to settle lawsuits filed by victims of the San Bruno blast. Criminal prosecutions in such cases are rare because they require proof that company managers knowingly disregarded federal safety rules.[9] In fact, the managers had been repeatedly informed about leaks by San Bruno residents, and they had indeed *knowingly* disregarded safety considerations—and continued to do so long after the explosion. Here was a familiar regulatory (or nonregulatory) pattern that has been repeated with numerous agencies in numerous states. There is one set of rules for average citizens and another for big, rich business firms.

By 2013 the PUC state regulators unanimously and compliantly approved a two-year PG&E rate increase of almost $300 million to help pay for pipeline inspection and upgrade costs. The ratepayers will ultimately be footing 55 percent of long-term safety costs.[10] The message being sent to PG&E was: Don't worry, your customers will be paying for your outrageous blunders, your suspiciously faulty records, and your misused or misplaced funds. And each time another disaster comes along, you can just jack up your monthly rates in service to your shareholders and managers at the expense of your ratepayers who have no choice but to get their gas and electricity from your flimsily regulated, private, for-profit, monopoly service.

At the same time, there remained a sixty-year-old state law backed by all the private utilities in California. This law bars citizens from obtaining government records about the safety of pipelines running underneath their neighborhoods. Records on gas pipeline accidents, electrocutions, and utility fires have also been withheld. "Everything is secret unless it is declared otherwise," proclaimed Frank Lindh, general counsel for the Public Utilities Commission. Lindh knows of what he speaks. Before coming to represent the public by working for the commission, he was a lawyer for PG&E.[11]

Not in the Safety Business

Throughout the United States people are at risk from improperly maintained gas lines belonging to private utilities that go largely unsupervised and unpunished. Average fines for injuries to self and damages to homes are less than $30,000 and not easily collected.

PG&E's CEO, Peter Darbee, formerly of Goldman Sachs, reassured the public that he was "focused on the tragedy" in San Bruno and on "how best to respond to the authorities involved." Darbee said nothing about his profit-driven leadership and his conviction that the utility was not in the safety business.[12] Like so many big corporations, PG&E does what it can to cut corners on maintenance and safety. The lower the maintenance costs, the higher the profits. The corroding pipelines fit well into the bigger picture, as part of the corroding infrastructure of the entire public sector.

Contrary to what business firms claim, safety is not a prime concern for giant corporations, if any concern at all, because safety does not bring in any money. Safety tests, supervisory inspections, repairs, reinforcements, and other such services cost money and cut into profits. Companies are continually looking for ways to skimp on safety maintenance. Like any other multibillion-dollar firm, PG&E is first and foremost in the business of making the highest possible payouts to its shareholders and its executives. The system works just fine for those whose real job is to skim the cream, those who do not have to pay the costs. That is the alpha and omega of modern corporate capitalism itself.

Lives were lost in San Bruno; homes were totally obliterated. Many who did not lose their lives or their health lost all their life possessions. Darbee and his cohorts should be facing jail sentences instead of golden parachutes. Even the *Contra Costa Times*—no radical broadsheet—urged the PUC "not to allow PG&E to raise rates to cover the expense of the San Bruno explosion or the cost of doing more and better pipe inspections. These costs should be borne by PG&E managers, employees, and investors."[13] Instead these costs are to be passed on to ratepayers and taxpayers.

Along with PG&E are other private utilities that seem to treat safety and other costs as something that the public—not the private company—should worry about. Thus, in 2013, Southern California Edison Co. repeatedly ran advertisements in local papers to make the case that customers must help pay for the closing and cleanup of the San Onofre nuclear power plant. Edison was attempting to shift the plant's decommissioning costs from its shareholders to its ratepayers.[14]

Earlier, in 2004, Southern California Edison spent $770 million to replace two aging steam generators with new models that were supposed to last twenty years—but were shut down after just twenty months. As of 2014 the whole plant was permanently closed. Ratepayers of Edison and a San Diego utility (also a private one) continued to pay for power they were not getting—from a plant that was not running. They also paid for replacement power amounting to nearly $1 billion in one year. Edison wanted the PUC to delay any decision on reducing rates until 2016.[15] So much for the superior performance of for-profit corporations. In 2013 Edison applied with PUC to raise its customers' rates from 2015 to 2017, for a cumulative increase of $841 million (or 12.4 percent) in that three-year period.

While all this was going on, another private corporation in the energy business, Chevron, was wreaking havoc upon the commonweal. In Richmond, California, a forty-year-old pipe in an oil refinery failed and caused an explosion that sent a huge plume of black smoke into the air and drove more than 9,000 people to the emergency rooms of area hospitals. A lawsuit filed by a group of victims listed thirteen Richmond refinery fires and hazardous releases of chemicals into the atmosphere from 1989 to 2012. One lawyer for the plaintiffs complained about the weakly enforced (or unenforced) regulatory controls that the corporations repeatedly disregard: "The process of government regulators isn't working. If it was, these fires wouldn't keep happening."[16]

The California PUC eventually fined PG&E $14.4 million for failing to notify regulators about incorrect records on a natural gas pipeline running through the city of San Carlos. According to one PUC commissioner, the substantial fine was designed to serve as a deterrent to similar behavior in the future. This was to let PG&E know that it had to produce "forthright and timely disclosure in all matters of public safety."

Left out of the whole picture is how corporate malfeasance and corporate-generated disasters are a reflection of the neoliberal capitalist system. If a gas pipeline had exploded in communist Cuba, let us say, killing people and destroying homes, the incident would have immediately been treated by US commentators as evidence of the deficiencies of the broader economic structure, a "dysfunctional" socialist system, proof that socialism cannot do it right. But disasters in our own corporate capitalist society are seen simply as isolated mishaps. At worst they are treated as instances of negligence and mismanagement by a particular company in a local situation, never as the characteristic outcome of a profit-driven capitalist system that steadfastly puts profits before people, with immense costs (and disasters) passed along to the public. The same is true of mining accidents, train wrecks, plane crashes, unsafe vehicles, unsafe consumer products and foods, toxic spills, offshore-drilling calamities, and a host of other noxious things that corporate America foists upon us.

Profits Are the Raison d'Être

Pressed on the matter, the captains of corporate America might admit that their primary and sole objective is profit maximization. Steel magnate David Roderick once said that his company "is not in the business of making steel. We're in the business of making profits."[17] The social uses of the product and its effects upon human well-being and the natural environment win consideration in capitalist production, if at all, only to the extent that they do not intrude upon the company's profit goals.

Rather than spend money on replacing aging pipelines, PG&E—just three months before the San Bruno catastrophe—poured $46 million of ratepayer money (ten times the amount needed for repairing the San Bruno pipeline) into the statewide electoral campaign for Proposition 16. This proposition was designed to make it nigh impossible for local governments to purchase energy from alternative sources, impossible to get out from under PG&E's monopoly grip. Proposition 16 was miraculously defeated despite the corporation's immense outlay of campaign funds on the issue. The media bombardments boosting the (monopolistic) virtues of PG&E were to no avail. The public was not buying the utility's line.

With thousands of miles of aging pipes to inspect and probably replace, PG&E continues to find other things to do. Through most of 2010, it was busy putting "smart meters" into people's homes. The new meters did not need to be read by an employee out in the field. Instead data from residences and businesses were transmitted by a mesh network of radio signals.

Critics complained that the smart meters were too smart. They often inflated electric bills. Worse still, they were feared to be harmful to our health. There is evidence that radio-frequency exposure is linked to cancer and other diseases. A number of ratepayers already complained of being sickened by the heavy doses of radio-frequency from smart meters. PG&E gave reassurances that the frequencies posed no great danger, but the company continued to face community resistance and skeptical questions from independent investigators.[18]

The smart meters have cost ratepayers more than $2 billion. They have also cut labor costs. Lower labor costs do not bring lower rates for ratepayers but higher profits for managers and stockholders. Never accuse companies like PG&E of neglect or stupidity. The company knows what it is doing: Like all companies in a corporate capitalist system, PG&E exists not to serve the public but to serve itself. The goal is not to distribute gas and electricity. The goal is to make the highest possible profit for the corporation at whatever cost or risk to the general public that the company can get away with.

Energy companies may show little enthusiasm for bringing safety to the public; instead they are vigorously engaged in hydraulic fracturing (fracking). The reader might recall that fracking is the highly controversial process of shooting many hundreds of thousands of gallons of toxic chemicals and water into the ground in order to fracture underground shale deposits and reach natural gas deposits. PG&E is engaged in bringing large amounts of fracked natural gas to northern California. While portraying itself as a "green" utility, it was involved in a project that promised not only to ratchet up the growth of fracking but also threatened to inflate natural gas prices by 100 to 300 percent, at enormous cost to the public and great profit to PG&E.[19]

Many of us favor public ownership of utilities so that the company might serve the public rather than the super rich who are served so well at such great cost to the rest of us. A public utility would not have to spend large sums on advertising to pump up its profiteering. There would be no profiteering. A public utility does not pocket vast profits for its owners. It has no owners other than the general public. Instead it would channel such earnings into the public treasury to be used for needed repairs and improvements. There are numerous instances in which not-for-profit public ownership works so much better than profit-driven private ownership. Utilities are one such case.

To conclude, the discussion herein provides some vivid examples of the profit pathology operating at the company level:

- While PG&E, or any other firm, makes claim to serving the public, in fact it serves itself, that is, its executives and shareholders. Money supposedly slated for safety purposes was used in public relations campaigns to keep communities from turning to not-for-profit public energy sources.
- PG&E's disregard for safety regulations shows a total lack of social responsibility, a dehumanized mode of operation: profit over people, indeed profit over people's lives.
- Like so many other companies, PG&E is part of a corporate America that scorns the impoverished denizens who are "always looking for a handout." Yet, with their big campaign donations and thousands of lobbyists in Washington and in state governments, the paladins of corporate America hustle for handouts more than anyone else.
- Evading lifesaving regulations shows the corporation to be answerable only to itself, a form of corporate autocracy. "Ratepayers should not have to pay for PG&E's failure to properly inspect, test, repair, and keep records for its gas pipelines that led to the deadly San Bruno explosion."[20]
- Corporate America carries a pretense of efficiency. In fact, many times it functions with great waste and inefficiency and at great cost to the public.

In sum, our problems do not arise from a corporation's failure to fulfill its professed functions (for instance, providing safe and affordable gas and electricity) but from its success in filling its real functions: making profits at every turn so as to further enrich them that have.

5

Free Market Medicine
A Personal Account

When I went for surgery at Alta Bates Summit, a medical center and affiliate of Sutter Health in Berkeley, California, I discovered that legal procedures took precedence over medical ones. I also discovered a number of other things about free market medicine.

Self-Reliance the Rugged Way

I had to sign intimidating statements about financial counseling, indemnity, patient responsibilities, consent to treatment, use of mystifying electronic technologies, and the like. One of these documents committed me to the following: "The hospital pathologist is hereby authorized to use his/her discretion in disposing of any member, organ, or other tissue removed from my person during the procedure." *Any member? Any organ? Removed from my person?*

The following day I returned for the actual operation. While playing Frank Sinatra recordings, the surgeon went to work cutting open several layers of my abdomen in order to secure my intestines with a permanent mesh implant. Afterward I spent two hours in the recovery room. "I feel like I've been in a knife fight," I told one nurse. "It's called surgery," she said with a friendly smile.

Then, while still pumped up with anesthetics and medications, I was rolled out into the street. *The street?* Yes, some few hours after surgery they sent me home. In countries that have *socialized medicine* (there I said it), a van might be waiting with trained personnel to help you to your abode. Not so in free market America. Your presurgery agreement specifies in boldface that you must have "a responsible adult acquaintance" (as opposed to an irresponsible teenage stranger) take you home in a private vehicle. I kept thinking, what happens to those unfortunates who have no one to bundle them away? Do they languish endlessly in the hospital driveway until the nasty weather finishes them off? You are not allowed to call a taxi because were a taxi driver to cause you any harm, you could hold the hospital legally responsible. Again it is a matter of lawyers and liability, not doctors and health.

One of the friends who assisted in getting me home then went off to the pharmacy to buy the powerful antibiotics I had to take every four hours for two days. I dislike how antibiotics destroy the "good bacteria" that our bodies produce and depend upon and how they help create dangerous strains of super-resistant bacteria. I kept thinking of a recent finding: Excessive reliance on pharmaceutical drugs kills more Americans—some 100,000 per year—than all illegal narcotics combined.[1] Yet we hear very little about it.

Why, in the first place, did I have to take antibiotics? Because, as everyone kept telling me, hospitals are hugely unsafe places overrun with Staph infections and other super bugs. The antibiotics are a matter of self-preservation.

Two days after surgery I noticed a dark red discoloration on my lower abdomen indicating internal bleeding. I was supposed to get a follow-up call from a nurse who would check on how I was doing. But the call might never come because the staff was planning a walkout. "We have no contract," one of them told me when I was in the recovery room. So now the nurses were going out on strike—and I was left on my own to divine what my internal bleeding was all about.

Fortunately, it did not turn out that way. A nurse did call me despite the walkout. Yes, she said, it was internal bleeding, but it was to be expected. My surgeon, bless him, called later in the day to confirm this opinion. Death was not yet knocking.

Fighting with the Medical Industry

A few days later, there were massive nurse strikes against Sutter on both coasts. Among other things, the nurses were complaining about "being disrespected by a corporate hospital culture that demands sacrifices from patients and those who provide their care, but pays executives millions of dollars."[2] One cold-blooded Sutter management negotiator was quoted as saying, "We have the money. We just don't have the will to give it to you."[3]

Sutter Health has centers in more than one hundred northern California cities and towns. As a "not-for-profit" company, Sutter pays no property taxes to California or any of the state's municipalities, and no corporate taxes to the federal government. Sutter proudly anoints itself the "price leader" in California's health care industry. It boasts about having "successfully cut costs and raised profits," showing other California health providers the way "to increase their prices and profits"[4]—which is what free market health care is all about.

As an affiliate of Sutter, Alta Bates Summit Medical Center follows the practice of putting the squeeze on its employees, having fewer personnel tending to more patients. In early 2014, Alta Bates decided to slash 358 positions, including employees at its skilled nursing facility.[5] In recent years, Sutter has faced strong criticism from labor unions, consumer groups, insurers, and others for its tight wages and high prices. The company claims it is "only trying to stay competitive."

This is how health care is sold on the free market: at runaway prices getting higher every year, accompanied by a mean squeeze on workforce wages. Charges for common in-patient procedures go only in one direction: upward. Some hospital costs have climbed yearly at *more than four times* the normal national rate of inflation, according to data released by Medicare officials.[6] Little if any of these ever increasing rates are redistributed to the caregivers. Consider the doctors. Both my surgeon and my general practitioner (GP) are among the victims, not the perpetrators, of today's corporate medical system. My GP explained that it was nigh impossible to get insurance companies to pay for services they supposedly cover. Feeling less like a doctor and more like a bill collector, he found he could no longer engage in endless telephone and email struggles with uncooperative insurance companies.

There are 1,500 medical insurance companies in America, all madly dedicated to maximizing profits by increasing premiums and withholding payments. The medical industry in toto is the nation's largest and most profitable business, with an annual take of more than $1 trillion. Along with the giant insurance and giant pharmaceutical companies, the greatest profiteers are the health maintenance organizations (HMOs), notorious for charging steep monthly payments while underpaying their staffs and requiring their doctors to spend less time with each patient, sometimes even withholding necessary treatment.

I myself am without private insurance. And my Medicare goes just so far. Like many other doctors, my GP no longer accepts Medicare or any insured patients. For a number of years now, Medicare payments to physicians have remained relatively unchanged while costs of running a practice have steadily increased. So now my GP's patients have to pay in full upon every visit, which for many of us is not easy—or even possible—to do.

Class Care

Our health system mirrors our class system. At the base of the pyramid are the very poor. Many of them suffer through long hours in emergency rooms only to be turned away with a useless or harmful prescription. No wonder "the United States has the worst record among industrialized nations in treating preventable deaths."[7] Recent reports show that hospitals still overcharge the poor. The Affordable Care Act (ACA, Obamacare) was supposed to rectify that situation. The "chargemaster" at many hospitals is "a list of hugely inflated prices that no one could explain or defend." And as of early 2014, with the ACA in place, there still were "no restraints on hospital bill collections or chargemaster charges for the neediest patients."[8]

Health care is one thing; health *coverage* is another. The for-profit health coverage system buries patients in mountains of red tape. To provide coverage, there are premiums to consider, along with copayments, waivers, rate hikes, surcharges, service charges, exclusions, late fees, and markups. Hospital billing varies wildly. In one Dallas hospital, the average charge for treating simple pneumonia was $14,600, while another Dallas hospital averaged more than $38,000 for the same treatment. A medical center in Arkansas charged $15,524 for a surgical spine fusion while the same operation at Temple University Hospital in Philadelphia averaged $219,273.[9] At times, identical treatments in the *very same hospital* may result in strikingly different bills. "The uninsured have virtually no bargaining power, which is why they are expected to pay much more" than others in the same hospital.[10]

Free market medicine has devolved into an inequitable, perilous feeding frenzy, often leaving the very poor with no care at all. The indigent simply die of whatever illness assails them because they cannot afford treatment: the free market in inaction. An acquaintance of mine told me how her mother died of AIDS because she could not afford the medications that might have kept her alive. In Houston I once got talking with a limousine driver, a young African American man, who remarked sadly that both his parents had died of cancer without ever receiving any treatment. "They just died," he said.

Living just above the poor in the class pyramid are the much-admired and much-pitied middle-class denizens. Despite the Affordable Care Act, their medical burdens seem not to have lightened all that much, in some cases not at all. They watch medical coverage disappear while paying out costly amounts to the profit-driven insurance companies.

I was able to get surgery at Alta Bates only because I was old enough to have Medicare and had enough disposable income to meet the copayment. For my outpatient hernia operation, the hospital charged Medicare $19,466. Of this, Medicare paid $2,527. And I was billed $644. The hospital then wrote off the unpaid portion. Had I no Medicare coverage, I would have had to pay the entire $19,466. I was informed by the hospital that this larger amount covers only hospital costs for equipment, technicians, supplies, and room. So besides the $644, I will have to pay for any pathologists, surgical assistants, and anesthesiologists who performed additional services. I waited in my middle-class home for the other shoe to drop.

Who is pocketing all the money that is pulled in by the health industry? Not the doctors. Working for Sutter, my surgeon makes about $400 to $500 for the hernia operation performed on me. This includes everything: my pre-op and post-op visits and the surgery itself, an exacting undertaking that requires skills of the highest order. He also has to maintain insurance, an office, an assistant, and an increasing load of paperwork. My surgeon pointed out to me, "If you ask people how much I make on an operation like yours, they will say $4,000 to $5,000, and be wrong by a factor of ten." He noted that in a recent speech President Obama criticized a surgeon for charging $30,000 to replace a knee cap. "The surgeon gets a minute fraction of that amount," my doctor assured me.

Almost all the big money in the health care racket goes to insurance executives and hospital executives. They outstrip doctors' earnings by more than three to one at places like Sutter Health, where general physicians' annual salary averages $185,000 and that of hospital executives is $600,000. But the gap is many times greater when we consider the additional nonsalary compensations commonly handed out to top executives. Thus the chief executive of Aetna earned a salary of approximately $977,000 in 2012 but a total compensation package of more than $36 million, the bulk from stocks vested and options. A former president of Barnabas Health of New Jersey earned a total compensation of $21.7 million that same year.[11]

To make matters worse, there was talk about cutting Medicare payments to physicians by 27 percent. If this happens, it will be increasingly difficult to find a surgeon who takes Medicare. Still worse, the private insurance companies will join in squeezing the physicians for still more profits.

I was able to meet my payment of $644 not only because my operation was heavily subsidized by Medicare but because it was a one-day "ambulatory surgery." I fear how I would do if I had to undergo prolonged and extremely costly treatment.

Medical Mess and Money Madness

Those who claim that the US medical system is the greatest in the world should take a sober look. A 2012 Institute of Medicine report concludes that Americans spend upwards of a third of their health care dollars on tests, medications, excessive surgeries, and other procedures and administrative expenditures that do nothing to improve health outcomes. As one noted cancer surgeon writes, "We have a quiet epidemic of unnecessary, costly, and sometimes harmful medical care."[12]

Medical errors, for both inpatient and outpatient, have become the leading cause of death among Americans, exceeding cancer and heart ailments. Some 800,000 deaths per year are due to misdiagnosis, excessive radiation, unnecessary or poorly rendered surgeries, harmful pharmaceuticals, and other such things.[13] Most of these deaths are due to systemic causes rather than just individual mistakes by health care workers and individual doctors. They are the consequence of for-profit care: poor staff-patient ratios, excessive reliance on shift work, and a lack of follow-up inspections of procedures. For-profit hospitals have fewer examinations, more premature releases, fewer skilled staff, and fewer cleanup staff, resulting in a persistently higher medical mishap rate than found in nonprofit hospitals. The epidemic of dangerous hospital infections is largely due to insufficient cleansing procedures. If you think unbridled capitalism is always best, here is a chilling statistic: *"For-profit hospitals have two to four times the medical error rate as not-for-profit facilities."*[14]

The plutocrats are transforming the medical device industry into another great source of profit. In 2012 the industry engaged in an aggressive lobbying campaign to minimize the testing of medical devices and other high-risk medical products. The quicker these devices and drugs can be brought to market, the greater are the profits. Patient safety is an ever lesser consideration when measured against corporate gain.[15]

Many pharmaceutical products doled out to children are in dosages that have been measured only for adults. Children and adults can react quite differently to the same drug. Differences in weight, muscle, bone, water, protein, and fat can cause problems that are serious and even deadly. "Most of the time, when we're treating children, we don't know if we have the right drug, how safe it is, and what the right dose is," concludes one honest doctor.[16]

Hospitals often perform unnecessary—but very profitable—surgeries. These surgeries can introduce costly, preventable complications and infections. On an average of forty times a week US surgeons operate on the wrong patient or wrong body part.[17] A code of silence is likely to prevail regarding mishaps, including fatal ones.

State medical boards do next to nothing when it comes to patrolling malpractices like wrong-site surgeries, mislabeled patient specimens, lethal overdoses of medications, and infections caused by slipshod hygiene practices. Treatments are pushed upon patients who are at the end of their lives, treatments that are futile and miserable for the patient but profitable for the hospital.[18] In most hospitals patients are obliged to pay individually for each service and each test and procedure, from blood tests to ultrasound scans to minor medications. This means Americans tend to get more of everything whether necessary or not, regardless of questions of health and recovery, and at the highest prices going.[19]

Medical Luxury

Far above the shaky middle class, at the pinnacle of the class pyramid, are the 1 percent, those who do not have to worry about most of the problems and practices we have already mentioned: *the super rich*, those who have money enough for all kinds of state-of-the-art treatments at the very finest therapeutic centers around the world, complete with luxury suites with gourmet menus.

Among the medically privileged are members of Congress, Supreme Court justices, and the US president and their respective families. These leaders are treated at top-grade facilities, yet they pay nothing: They enjoy *socialized medicine.* No conservative lawmakers have held fast to their free market principles by refusing to accept this publicly funded, socialistic medical treatment for themselves and their families.

Jim Hightower noted that hospitals from New York to Los Angeles (often so overcrowded that regular patients end up on gurneys in the hallway) have set aside entire floors for deluxe suites that come with butlers, five-star meals, marble baths, and other amenities for the super rich. In these instances it is not medical care the hospitals are providing "but the personal pampering that the super rich expect in all aspects of their lives." These same hospitals draw huge subsidies from taxpayers. Hightower concludes, "It's repugnant for the plutocratic elite to pervert health care into a luxury commodity."[20] John Mackey, billionaire CEO of Whole Foods, disagrees: He cheerfully announced that medical care is not a human right; it should be "market determined just like food and shelter." Nobody has a higher opinion of John Mackey than I, and I think he is a greed-driven bloodsucker. Nevertheless I will give him credit for candidly admitting his dedication to a dehumanized profit pathology. For him and others who own the wealth of this nation, health care is a marketed commodity to be produced and sold only to those who can pay for it.

One report of health care in industrial nations showed the British National Health Service in Britain was vastly superior to what is found in the United States. In fact, US health care was ranked both the most expensive and the worst.[21] The US medical system costs many times more than what is spent in socialized systems, but it delivers much less in the way of quality care and cure. That's the way it is intended to be. The goal of any free market service—be it utilities, housing, transportation, education, or health care—is not to maximize performance but to maximize profits, often at the expense of performance. If profits are high, then the system is working just fine—for the 1 percent. But for us 99 percent, the lust for profit is the heart of the problem.

6

Free Market Medicine
More True Stories

WHEN I RECORDED MY PERSONAL EXPERIENCES with for-profit health care, the story elicited responses from readers who had their own accounts to share. Their testimonies add an additional dimension to the issue and deserve some attention.

Health care in the United States is hailed by conservative boosters as "the best medical system in the world." This has become one of the dubious mantras chanted again and again by the Fox News propagandists whenever the question of improving health care arises. Launching a tireless campaign against affordable health care, the Fox commentators conveniently confuse health care *cost* with health care *quality*. The US health care system certainly is the most *expensive*, most *profitable*, and most *complicated* system in the world, leaving millions of Americans in shock and desperation. But that does not make it the best, not by far.

Of the people who wrote to me, not one had anything positive to say about the US health system. Either they are chronic grouches or they are onto something. Below are their comments.[1]

Here is the very first email I received in response to my account about my hernia operation; it contains a familiar story:

> In the mid-90s I had an attack of sciatica while visiting relatives in the Bay Area. I went to Alta Bates Emergency. After I waited three hours, a doctor stopped by, saw me for two minutes, gave me a pain prescription and sent me home.
> Total bill was over $1,000.
>
> —*Marc Steinfeld*

Price gouging is the name of the game:

> I had a kidney stone which was causing me great pain. I drove myself to the emergency ward where I was told the kidney stone was so large that it had to be "shattered." I spent one night in the hospital. The operation was performed early the next morning. My family had to come pick me up, which they did by noon that same day. I wasn't even in the hospital for 24 hours. Imagine my shock when the bill came. It was $57,000, not including the doctor's bill! I actually thought it was a typo. I thought they had put the comma in the wrong place. Even $5,700 would have been quite a charge.
>
> After much hassle, Blue Cross settled with the hospital, except for $2,500 which I had to pay. Then Blue Cross promptly dumped me.
>
> —*Angela Robinson*

Collecting money from the sick and dying seems to be of far greater importance than trying to save and comfort them:

> I live in Minnesota, which is supposed to have such a great health care system. But when my Mom was dying of cancer Allina Health called her 2–3 times a day demanding to be paid in full. She had insurance and Medicare but they wanted their money right now. It was a campaign of harassment against someone who was dying. I had to call the attorney general's office to get it to stop. I couldn't believe it.
> —*Richard Cleland*

In my original article, I did not have much to say about pharmaceutical costs, but this next reader does:

> Medicare cannot negotiate drug prices, which means that the one Rx I take costs over $700 every three months, of which I pay $90 until I reach the "donut hole," which happens with just this one drug.[2] When I first started on this medication, the cost was about $350, so it has doubled in just three years. No improvements; it's the same exact drug and there are no generics. The only change is the higher price!
> Speaking of higher prices, I just renewed my prescription and the three month cost has increased again, from $718 to $781. My doctor at Kaiser said that should I get into the "donut hole" she would give me a prescription I can use at a Canadian pharmacy. It's crazy that even with a drug coverage plan, I'll eventually have to buy from a Canadian pharmacy!
> —*Judy Abbot Townley*

A subject deserving of more attention is iatrogenic disaster:

> The US medical/hospital/industrial system as it has developed is horrifying to me. I went through the hospital and nursing home

process with my late parents in the 90s up through 2000 when my mother died from an infection from an antibiotic resistant strain of bacteria, Mercer [MRSA], caught in the hospital.

At least you [Parenti] were not subject to staying overnight and having to endure a hospital food system which is criminally poor in nutritional value. . . . Plus the added risk of fatal infection.

—*Howard Goldman*

Here is another tragic mishap:

When the nurses went on strike at Alta Bates, a friend of mine was being treated for her uterine cancer, which was finally in remission. But the replacement nurse misdiagnosed the treatment and connected a tube in an erroneous way. My friend tragically died from the mishap. Such a sweet, wonderful person taken by medical error.

So, my friend, you [Parenti] were basically lucky that you got through your hernia operation and got out with your life intact. [My wife] recently had a small procedure and she is still getting bills from the treatment—six months later. In other words, you are right, always be prepared for "the other shoe to drop."

—*Roberto Ronaldi*

A noted author and friend of mine (whose real name is not used herein) reported on his medical treatment much as it was happening. Here is a composite of his communications to me. His medical treatment proved fatal:

Feeling that my neuropathy was worse, I called Dr. Seymour Rogov, head neurologist at [a New York] hospital. He put a long electrical needle into my leg muscle, and said I certainly had peripheral neuropathy. He gave me all sorts of medicines and started the IVIG, which apparently weakened my potassium and magnesium, both of which are most needed to build up heart muscles.

The IVIG that Rogov injected into me for five nights, every three hours, created tremendous side effects: pushing my previously normal blood pressure to as high as 208/101; also tremendous swelling of my feet, with one huge bubble on my right foot. It drooled a lot of water. When I returned home, I had to hold walls or walker. A new bubble formed on my left leg. Rogov told me I had spinal stenosis, which caused all my problems. Obviously he never looked at the medical file I had given him. I've had spinal stenosis since 1967.

Ten days later I happened to be due for my prostate exam at a different hospital. The MDs panicked over my blood pressure, and gave me leg scans, nuclear bone scans, pelvic scans—but have yet to give me results. They keep giving me potassium and magnesium but without giving any results. I was visited by lots of MDs who told me they had no idea what was wrong, except that I need to build up my weak potassium and magnesium to help my heart muscles which were weakened by the injections of IVIG.

A rude, insolent MD told me my whole problem was the Prostasol pills I got from a practitioner of Chinese medicine. This MD would not tell me his name. He kept repeating: it's my pills—which I have been taking since 1996 and which have kept my PSA under 30. No one ever died from PSA 30. This MD insisted that my pills are poison and are causing all my problems. He ordered(!) me to stop taking them.

My lawyers may go after Rogov for completely ruining my life and perhaps killing me. Remember that I was still on my feet teaching the day before I saw him.

[Several days later.] I can't keep it up. I cried today for the first time. Hospitals wear you down. They think they are efficient, but service is terrible. They do not treat the sores on my legs: "yes, yes, in a minute" that was two hours ago. They take blood not knowing they already did. They don't know any test results. But if I leave without their official discharge, I get no home care, no refunds from insurance or AARP. There's so many black-blue marks on my arms from all the injections, you can't see my original skin. If I ask someone strolling by to please hand me that glass, the answer: "not my job."

[Two more days go by.] Now they want a new biopsy of my prostate cancer, the most painful of all tests. I am resisting, reminding them that they have not given me any results of all their previous tests.

Feel like a prisoner, cannot get service, completely ignored. Disgusting lunch, could not eat any of it. Yet I have gained 20 lbs. from the shit they have injected into my body. Worst part, I have no results from all the tests. I told the MDs that I'm having difficulties swallowing. No response from them.

—*Juan "Lipo" Serano [The author of this report died two weeks after this last letter]*

Medical care in America for the longest time has been all about owing, billing, and paying. This letter deals with events from fifteen years ago. (The writer is herself an MD who is on disability.)

I have had my own disastrous hospitalization. In 1997, I had private insurance that left a lot unpaid. The hospital ate some of the uncovered costs as a one-time-only concession, but the "extras" (anesthesiologist, radiologists, etc.) insisted on full payment. I went over the supplies billing and was shocked at the repetitions and also the waste. . . .

At that time almost all my income from workman's comp went to pay my insurance coverage. Within a couple of years I was unable to continue to afford being insured due to pre-existing conditions.

The whole thing was so traumatic, I couldn't even write about it, though I wanted to! And I signed myself out a day early because I felt unsafe due to the many errors of omission or neglect made in my 3 days there.

A problem which I could not prove was surgical or due to post-op neglect left me with one-and-a-half years of rehab, a limp, and continued hip pain which, by the way, was not the area that was to be addressed by the surgery—it was my neck! But they took some bone from my hip to fix the neck... and apparently, the hip ended up being less well connected to the rest of me afterwards. And that was free market medicine and worker's protection health benefits fifteen years ago.

—*Deb Rosen*

There is no limit to the price gouging by drug companies and insurance agencies, even more outrageous when compared with prices in Canada:

A friend of mine in El Paso has been fighting breast cancer the last three years. She went for her three-year check up. . . . She had been doing really well up to then. Her tests showed the cancer had spread to her liver and bones. That's when the doctor mentions the drug AFINATOR. He tells her this drug has shown some amazing results in liver and bone cancers. Remember, she has insurance. She calls her insurance company and they will not pay for THAT DRUG! She called me so upset. She found out that to pay for this drug out of pocket would cost her $10,000 per thirty-day or monthly supply. Jesus! $10,000 every month. I called a Canadian friend and asked about that drug. He said nine out of thirteen provinces provide that drug FREE to citizens. My head is still spinning, Michael. That's what insurance companies do with our lives. This is my friend's life.

—*Judy Planchard*

Among the hardest hit by the medical free market are the homeless. Here is a report from someone who works for Task Force for the Homeless:

Every day we house 500 to 700 homeless Atlantans [Georgia], who are men, mostly. We distribute mail daily as well, and the bulk of the mail is hospital bills from our former charity hospital, which is now a private hospital. Homeless men who owe that hospital for treatment are often denied jobs and housing because of their credit problems. We are in the process of fighting those bills. All too often, our friends don't even seek treatment because they know they cannot pay. The prescriptions at that same hospital cost $10 each, and so people who take more than one medication often go without, as in the case of one man who had heart failure [and needed] life-saving medication.

—*Becky Walters*

In the previous chapter I mentioned that millions of low-income people must do without medical care entirely. A letter appearing in *Time* magazine brings it home:

I don't know whether to laugh or cry when hectored by well-meaning [doctors] to get regular cancer screenings. I am 62 with a part-time job and no health insurance. How am I to pay for tests? And if cancer is discovered, what on earth can I, and the many people like me, do about it?

—*Annette Harper*[3]

In a world ruled by corporate America, an injured worker can be discarded like a piece of trash to suffer a lifetime of pain and inadequate treatment:

> For years I lived as a hard-working bee in our society and the minute I got disabled and became unable to work in my field, the company disregarded my workers' comp claim. My back is disabled and I was in severe pain without ability to walk for about a year. I see now that if I had lived in a country with Public Option Healthcare, I could have gotten the care I needed without having to deal with AIG denial of my injury.[4] Once I got an attorney, things changed, but I still never received all my treatment for my back and received very little to compensate the daily handicap.
>
> I see now that I was subhuman and not worthy of proper medical attention and respect for the work I labored which ended in lifelong injury. I was exploited and my labors were useless to me and only useful to the company while I continued to be exploited. Did you know, I even let them coerce me to break Department of Transportation hours of service laws when I had to drive another twenty-hour shift with only a few hours off after a twenty-five-hour shift? We are nothing to the authoritarians but a means to make them rich on our sweat and blood.
>
> —*Wilfred J. Kennsington*

One of my readers offers a look at the Swiss system:

> Last year I had four eye surgeries and breast cancer and the maximum I paid was 7000 CHF [Swiss franc] for it all. I had to fight to get out of the hospital after five days because they wanted to make absolutely sure I had no problem with drainage. I was able to

walk out (no wheelchairs). A portion of my insurance payment does go to cover people who can't afford insurance. I'm fine with that.

I had a team that still keeps tabs on me and a lead nurse who is there 24/7. (When she has time off, a substitute is there for whatever I need.)

No way would I ever live in the US again. It's too cruel. I do carry insurance so that if I were in the US and I get sick, I get air "freighted" back to a civilized society.

—*Donna Peterson*

From a friend in Canada:

I am just appalled reading your account [about medical care in the United States]—although our Conservative government is trying very hard to destroy our cherished health care system these days. But to give you a personal example, my husband just had a total hip replacement and is due for another one this summer. Five years ago he had a serious bowel operation which required a nine-day stay at the hospital.

NO bills were sent to us for either of these operations. It is all included in our health care system OHIP for Ontario, the Ontario Health Insurance Plan.

The only cost this time is for buying a commode chair, a bath bench, and a walker (which we could have rented). And we will be able to deduct these expenses on our income taxes. We also have a $100 deductible yearly for our medications so it cost us about $6 to $8 for each prescription.

—*Marie Pierre St. Clare*

From another friend in Canada. After giving a detailed account of the excellent free treatment accorded her mother, she added:

Far too many Americans accept an utterly depraved and bizarre system of health-care-for-profit. The health system in the US is an aberration. Many Americans have been led to think that we Canadians pay a fortune for our health care in taxes. But Americans already pay more per capita in taxes for health care (that most of you don't receive) than do Canadians. We get full, FREE coverage, no questions asked.

Our system is under attack by the Conservatives. But so far, only free prescription drugs have been taken away from my Mum's coverage. She now pays about 20 percent of the cost of her heart medications. Until about a decade ago they were totally free of charge.

Meanwhile, my fellow Canadians are being lied to, and many are being hoodwinked. They look at the TV commercials for American for-profit health care, and listen to Fox television and its Canadian counterpart, Sun television, and the ranting of Prime Minister Steven Harper, and conclude that we [Canadians] have an inferior system.

—Alicia Hopkins

These observations from a friend in England:

I just read your article; a lot of it left me speechless. Some I am not surprised by; my friends in California have told me about their own horror stories when it comes to accessing health care. The National Health Service [in the United Kingdom] is far from perfect but we had peace of mind when a family friend had surgery recently and was taken to and from the hospital by mini-bus—so different from your experience.

—Gia Parker

We don't hear much about Slovakia but, judging from what a Slovakian friend of mine observed, the country's health system still has some communitarian traits carried over from earlier socialist days:

> Recently I cut my hand and it got infected, and blew up like an orange. I went to the emergency room. They took me immediately. They opened the swollen area and cleaned it with disinfectants and then they bandaged it thoroughly. The procedure did not take long, and it cost me two Euros (about $2.70 at that time).
>
> We have the newest dental technology from Switzerland. The dentist made a new cap for my tooth; it cost 250 Euros (about $332). Doctors and dentists charge "normal prices" and still they live quite well. In Slovakia when you feel sick, let's say you have a fever or you're vomiting or you cannot walk from illness, within ten minutes emergency comes directly to your home. And you pay something very little.
>
> People in Eastern Europe complain about medical care but it's not bad compared with your system. I pay 56 Euros a month for insurance, then one Euro for each doctor's visit. Here in Slovakia for minor treatments you don't pay anything to speak of.
>
> —*Frieda Mangova*

In sum, readers found health-care practices in the United States to be quite unsettling. The above comments indicate that many people in the United States have a story of their own to tell about the profit-driven medical industry. And people abroad make clear to us that their socialized or quasisocialized medical systems are more humane and less cruel than the for-profit plunder that is the US system—even if the European medical systems also sometimes suffer from faulty practices and ruthless cutbacks by conservative governments.

Finally, it is worth repeating: The corporate goal in the United States and some other places is to treat medical care not as a human right but as a market-determined profit-driven service, increasingly expanding in cost. We should unequivocally demand socialized medicine, that is, a publicly funded and publicly administered system whose purpose is human care rather than profit accumulation. It would provide very good salaries for caregivers, including doctors, and would cost so much less while serving us so much better.

Part Three

Cultural Aberrations and Other Oppressions

7

Pedophiles, Popes, Priests, Preachers, and Papa

THOSE AT THE APEX OF THE SOCIAL PYRAMID enjoy a vast reach of power and prestige. They and their hired staffs propagate the iconic figures and narratives that are intended to be revered by the multitude. The Übermensch, the privileged few, lords over the rest of us with something close to impunity. Given their weaker position in the social order, selected victims from the vulnerable multitude may be subjected to all sorts of abuses. Some of these abuses are so shocking as to enjoy the cover of incredulity. That is to say, the general public simply will not believe what they hear.

Objectification and Victimization

The exploitation of the weak by the stronger can be found within personal relations as well as institutional relations. Objectification happens when a person becomes an instrument of another's unjust and exploitative desires. The objectified person is the disadvantaged one, usually economically dependent, a weaker product of the patriarchal socioeconomic order. Of course, objectification can be found in any hierarchical, elitist society that thrives on autocratic exploitation. With objectification, "the CEO is more apt at seeing employees as numbers on a spreadsheet, the banker is able to view clients as nothing more than borrowers, the landlord is able to view a family simply as renters, and the boss sees nothing but workers who need to be prodded like cattle. . . . The objectifiers, through the process of dehumanizing the objectified, become less human themselves."[1]

Frequently this exploitative objectified relationship can be replicated in a religious setting, one that even involves sexual exploitation, as when holy and privileged keepers of sectarian groups prey upon the most defenseless of their trusting flock, an age-old subterranean crime finally exposed in the last few decades in the United States and around the world.

The sexual victims most easily preyed upon usually are not yet fully matured, physically or mentally, and are wanting in personal defenses and social resources. They frequently are children or institutional subordinates, or both. Along with the special susceptibilities of childhood, they might endure such deficiencies as poverty, hunger, disability, and dependency, making them ready targets when encountering conniving superordinates. The elderly poor are also among those who suffer a pronounced financial and physical vulnerability. But here we will focus on the children who have so long been treated like fair game.

Sexual predators often occupy positions of esteem and trust in their communities: priests, ministers, rabbis, imams, teachers, gurus, therapists, police officers, day care supervisors, reformatory attendants, doctors, coaches, celebrities, adult relatives (especially fathers), and others. Predators seek out situations that afford opportunities for *pedophilia*, the sexual abuse of children by adults.

In social structures predicated on maximizing inequality, the disadvantaged pay dearly. Children (along with many women and some men) risk having their bodies and souls repeatedly violated. With sex trafficking and indentured servitude, children and women are victimized at both levels: forced sexuality and forced labor.

Pedophilia is categorized not as an illness but as a crime, and with good reason. Children seldom have the means to resist predators. Frequently the violators convince themselves that their victims are freely consenting. They conveniently forget that a vulnerable child cannot give free and full consent to an intimidating adult. Such encounters can have a toxic impact in the victims' later life in the form of depression, eating disorders, nightmares, sexual dysfunction, drug addiction, and even suicide.

Roman Catholic priests do not have a monopoly on pedophilia. If anything, the highly publicized charges of child rape and molestation among the Catholic clergy has made us additionally aware of the pedophilic abuses perpetrated also by other people in an exploitative society that commodifies almost everything, including children. But let us begin with the priests and popes.

See No Evil

When Pope John Paul II was still living in Poland as Cardinal Karol Wojtyła, he complained that the security police would accuse priests of sexual abuse just to hassle and discredit them.[2] For him, the Polish pedophilia problem was nothing more than a communist plot to smear the church. Or perhaps the pope was perfectly aware of the abusive practices going on among some clergy and was simply covering up for them by laying blame on the already demonized communists.

In recent years, clerical abuse cases have been slowly surfacing in postcommunist Poland. Writing in the leading daily *Gazeta Wyborcza*, a middle-aged man reported having been sexually abused as a child by a priest. He acknowledged, however, that Poland was not prepared to deal with such transgressions. "It's still too early. . . . Can you imagine what life would look like if an inhabitant of a small town or village decided to talk? I can already see the committees of defense for the accused priests." By 2013–2014, however, Poland's influential Catholic Church was hit by a series of child abuse charges. One pedophile priest was sentenced to 8.5 years in prison. At his trial, sure enough, dozens of parishioners showed up to defend their priest, who had pleaded not guilty.[3]

Today we have a mountainous sludge of pedophilic revelations spanning numerous nations, going back decades or, as some historians maintain, even centuries.[4] By the early 1980s, now ensconced in Rome as Pope John Paul II, Wojtyła treated all reports about pedophile clergy as little more than slander against the church. This remained the pontiff's unwavering stance for the next twenty years. The pope strenuously ignored the complaints targeting one of his favorites: Rev. Marcial Maciel, founder of an oddly sinister religious order called the Legion of Christ. "Marcial Maciel established a cult of abuse and coverup," declared one of the former seminarians who filed a canonical lawsuit charging Maciel with having assaulted and raped about twenty seminarians and a large number of children.[5] Years later, an AP story carried excerpts from more than two hundred Vatican documents regarding sexual assaults and use of drugs by Maciel. John Paul refused to acknowledge these charges and continued to hail Maciel as an "efficacious guide to youth."[6] In 2006, after the pope died, Maciel was allowed a comfortable retirement.

For decades church superiors ignored complaints about pedophile priests. Accused clerics were quietly bundled off to distant congregations where they could resume preying upon children of unsuspecting parishioners. This practice of denial, concealment, and rotation has been so consistently pursued in nation after nation as to leave the impression of being a deliberate church policy. To this day, the Vatican expects church officials to inform secular authorities about sexual assault cases only "if required by local law." If not required by local law, then presumably there is no need to report these felonious crimes, and predators may prowl with impunity.

Instructions from Rome requiring bishops and cardinals to keep matters secret were themselves kept secret. The cover-up was itself covered up. John Paul specifically mandated that all charges against priests were to be reported secretly to the Vatican. Hearings were to be held *in camera*, a procedure that directly defies state criminal codes. Meanwhile, the pontiff continued to give safe haven to cardinals who had covered up abuse cases. He also continued to ignore requests to meet with groups of abuse survivors.

Rather than being defrocked, many predator priests have been moved into well-positioned posts as administrators, vicars, and parochial school officials, repeatedly accused by their victims while repeatedly promoted by their superiors. Church spokesmen have employed a vocabulary of compassion and healing—not for the children but for the pedophiles. They treat the rapist as a misdirected sinner who must be given a chance to confess his transgressions and mend his ways. This generously forgiving approach is of little therapeutic efficacy when dealing with pedophiles. A far more effective deterrent is the threat of an extended prison stay. Absent any risk of serious punishment, the perpetrator is restrained only by the availability of potential victims and the limits of his own appetite.

Forgiving No One Else

The church's responses to the crimes within its walls are typical of almost all hierarchical institutions and self-serving organizations that face scandal:

- Church leaders long refused to acknowledge the existence of such crimes. They ignored outcries from victims, parents, and staff. They sometimes blamed the victims themselves for inviting molestation (and still do). The hierarchy thereby becomes an accessory to the crime.
- Church leaders assured us that pedophilia was a rarity. They made light of pedophilic offenses, insisting that the padre was just being affectionate and had misjudged boundaries. At worst, the priestly predator is seen as a sinner who has strayed. The crime was treated only as a sin. Instead of incarceration, there is to be repentance and absolution. If the perpetrator had committed *murder*, it would have been reported to the police, we may presume. But pedophilia was not seen as a crime to be taken too seriously, much the way university authorities cover up campus rapes.
- For many years, the church hierarchs expurgated their records rather than hand them over to authorities, thereby aiding and abetting the predators. They also have repeatedly silenced the whistle-blowers within the church who have sided with the victims.
- The hierarchs sequester church funds in order to appear unable to pay compensations demanded in victims' lawsuits. Much of the church's announced settlement payments goes to its own lawyers and to abusive priests as an incentive to retirement.[7]

Clergy who struggled for social justice throughout Latin America and a number of other countries enjoyed none of the hierarchal protection doled out to the pedophile priests. No tolerance was extended by John Paul II to politically radical priests and nuns. He threw the Vatican's weight *against* liberation theology, replacing reform-minded bishops and clergy with conservative ones. He suppressed liberation theology curricula and silenced its theorists in Catholic educational institutions. And he ordered clergy to refrain from egalitarian secular political activities.[8]

John Paul II would not bother to remove clergy who raped children but he readily silenced clergy who advocated birth control and abortion, or who proposed that priests be allowed to marry, or who were tolerant of homosexuals, or who believed that women should be ordained into the priesthood.

Clergy who have spoken against child abusers in their ranks have had their careers shut down. As with many other institutions, so with the Catholic Church: Those who *expose* the deplorable behavior of institutional personnel are more readily targeted for punitive action than those who actually commit the deplorable acts. The whistle-blower, not the perpetrator, is subjected to retribution. The institutional superiors are far more concerned about the unfavorable publicity to the institution than about the criminal harm done to children.

A Law Unto Itself

Church leaders conveniently forget that pedophilia is a felony crime and that, as citizens of a secular state, priests are subject to the state's laws just like the rest of us. Clerical authorities have argued in court that criminal investigations of "church affairs" violated the free practice of religion guaranteed by the US Constitution—as if raping little children were a holy sacrament. Church officials are themselves guilty of obstructing justice when they refuse to talk to state authorities. They offer no pastoral assistance to young victims and their shaken families. They do not investigate to see if other children have been victimized by the same priests. And they sometimes threaten young plaintiffs with excommunication or countersuits.

Responding to charges that one of his priests sexually assaulted a six-year-old boy, Cardinal Bernard Law asserted that "the boy and his parents contributed to the abuse by being negligent."⁹ Law himself never went to prison for the hundreds of cover-ups he orchestrated. In 2004, with things getting too hot for him in his Boston archdiocese, Cardinal Law was rescued by John Paul II to head one of Rome's major basilicas, where he continued to live with diplomatic immunity in palatial luxury on a generous stipend.

A judge of the Holy Roman Rota, the church's highest court, wrote in a Vatican-approved article that bishops should refuse to release abusers' records to law enforcement authorities. He claimed that the confidentiality of their files came under the same legal protection as privileged communications in the confessional—a notion that has no basis in canon or secular law. Bishop James Quinn of Cleveland even urged church officials to send incriminating files to the Vatican Embassy in Washington, DC, where diplomatic immunity would prevent the documents from being subpoenaed.¹⁰

A Few Bad Apples?

Years ago the Catholic hierarchy insisted that clerical pedophilia involved just a few bad apples. John Paul II scornfully denounced the media for "sensationalizing" the issue. Vatican leaders directed more fire at news outlets for publicizing the crimes than at their own clergy for committing them.

After much publicity and pressure, the U.S. Conference of Catholic Bishops—to their credit—did release a report documenting sexual violations committed by 4,392 priests in America against thousands of children between 1950 and 2002. One of every ten priests ordained in 1970 was charged as a pedophile by 2002, and those were only the cases reported. Another survey commissioned by the bishops found that at least sixteen American *bishops* were perpetrators.¹¹ So much for a few bad apples.

Even as victim reports were flooding in from scores of other countries, John Paul II dismissed the pedophilic epidemic as "an American problem," as if this made it a matter of no great moment. John Paul II went to his grave in 2005 still refusing to voice any regrets regarding sex crimes and cover-ups in a variety of countries. As recently as May 2014, a UN panel criticized the Vatican for its failures to inform civil authorities about sexually abusive priests and its failure to ensure redress for victims.[12]

There are two ways we can think of child rape as not being a serious problem, and the Catholic hierarchy seems to have embraced both of these positions at various times. First, one can say pedophilia is not that serious if it involves only a few isolated and passing incidents. Second, an even more creepy way of downplaying the problem, one can say that the act of molestation simply is not all that important. At worst, it is unfortunate; it might upset the child for a spell, but it certainly is not significant enough to cause unnecessary scandal and ruin the career of an otherwise splendid padre who had succumbed to a passing temptation.

Church bigwigs have been remarkably indifferent toward the abused children. When one of the most persistent perpetrators, Rev. John Geoghan, was forced into retirement (not jail) after seventeen years and nearly two hundred victims, Cardinal Law could still write him, "On behalf of those you have served well, in my own name, I would like to thank you. I understand yours is a painful situation."[13] It is evident that Law was more concerned about the "pain" endured by Geoghan than the ruinous misery the priest had inflicted upon children.

A former top Vatican cardinal, Dario Castrillón, claimed that John Paul II had authorized a letter sent to bishops around the world, calling on them to resist the intrusions of civil authorities on matters relating to child abuse.[14] Castrillón (an active opponent of liberation theology) said that child abuse stemmed from "pan sexuality and sexual licentiousness" in America. He defended church laws that required dealing "with internal matters in an internal way."[15]

There are many like Cardinals Law and Castrillón in the hierarchy, aging reactionary men who have no life experience with children and show not the slightest empathy for them, though they do claim it their duty to protect the "unborn child." They live in an old-boys network, jockeying for power and position within an institution that feeds, shelters, and adorns them throughout their lives. From their heady heights, church leaders cannot hear the weeping victims. Their mighty church belongs not to little children but to the bedecked oligarchs who seem largely unruffled by predation.

Circling the Wagons

The Roman hierarchy managed to convince itself that the prime victim in this dismal saga was the church itself. The hierarchy circled the wagons against outside enemies who were "smearing" the church. Pope Benedict XVI, John Paul's successor, blamed "secularism" and misguided applications of Vatican II's aggiornamento as contributing to the pedophilia. Reform-minded liberalism made us do it, he seemed to be saying.

This bristling counterattack by the hierarchy did not play well with the public. Church authorities came off looking like insular arrogant elites who were unwilling to own up to a horrid situation within their ranks. Meanwhile bishops in Germany and Belgium were confessing to charges that they themselves had abused minors; and new allegations were arising in Ireland, Chile, Norway, Brazil, Italy, France, Mexico, and elsewhere.

Pope Benedict held brief meetings with survivor groups and issued sympathetic statements that many victims found to be too little, too late. If the Vatican really wanted to make amends, they argued, it should stop obstructing justice. It should ferret out abusive clergy and not wait until cases are publicized by others. And it should make public the church's many thousands of still secret reports on priests and bishops. In May 2014, the successor to Benedict, Pope Francis, announced that he would meet with victims and move against pedophilic clergy with "zero tolerance."[16]

Some courageous priests continued to speak out. At a Sunday Mass outside Springfield, Massachusetts, the Rev. James Scahill delivered a telling sermon to his congregation: "It is beginning to become evident that for decades, if not centuries, church leadership covered up the abuse of children and minors to protect its institutional image and the image of priesthood." The abusive priests, Scahill went on, were "felons." Vatican leaders should not claim innocent ignorance. They were either deceivers or incompetents who in either case "should resign." How did Father Scahill's conservative suburban Catholic parishioners receive his scorching remarks? One or two walked out. The rest gave him a standing ovation.[17]

Protestants, Jews, and Others

While focusing on the Catholic clergy, we should not downplay other denominations. There is the simpleminded presupposition that priests are driven to pedophilia because they are deprived of marriage as a sexual outlet. This can be put to rest by the prevalence of sex offenders among Protestant clerics, all of whom are married or allowed to marry. An investigation by victims' groups of this country's largest Protestant denomination, the Southern Baptists, discovered scores of sexual crimes charged against Baptist ministers (many married), with little being done about it.[18]

Ministers of a wide range of Protestant denominations have been charged with raping children. Rev. Eugene Paul White, Baptist minister in Orangevale, California, was convicted of sexually abusing his four adopted foster daughters from 1999 to 2004. White blamed the girls, ages eight to twelve, for deliberately enticing him.[19] Every month, an atheist publication, *Freethought Today*, promulgates lists of clergy of all denominations who are connected to a litany of crimes, including theft, embezzlement, fraud, burglary, drug trafficking, voyeurism, indecent exposure, sexual solicitation, and pedophilic violations of every variety.[20] Within Orthodox Jewish communities substantial numbers of rabbis have been charged with sexual crimes and attempts to cover them up. These cases have rarely been given attention in the mainstream media. One report cites more than fifty rabbis—along with additional Jewish counselors, doctors, therapists, teachers, and others—who molested children or committed related crimes.[21]

Under Hasidim rule there exists a proscription known as *Mesirah* (or *mesira*) that prohibits Jews from reporting other Jews to secular authorities, even when their conduct is a criminal violation of secular law. Rabbis who molest children often benefit from the impunity granted by this religious rule. Furthermore, a Jew who violates *Mesirah* law by informing on his fellow Jews is looked down upon by the ultra-Orthodox community and may no longer be protected by the Torah, the body of judgment and law contained in Jewish Scripture.[22]

The ultra-Orthodox community leadership in Brooklyn, New York, required their members to inform a rabbi before reporting accusations of pedophilia to the district attorney or the police. Victims and their families who have gone to the civil authorities have been subjected to harassment and intimidation by rabbinical leaders.[23] The Orthodox leaders have successfully silenced victims and covered up child-rape cases by attacking the victims and any Jew who aids them. One rabbi who assisted rape victims had a chemical thrown at his face and was grazed in the forehead by a shot from a pellet gun. For his good work on behalf of the victims, he was barred from local synagogues and formally ostracized by a group of religious judges.[24]

Regardless of *Mesirah*, more and more Hasidic families have begun to come forward with accounts of child victimization. Former students of Yeshiva University High School for Boys published accounts in the *Jewish Daily Forward* about molestation and abuse at the hands of the school's assistant principal, the Talmud teacher, and others in the 1980s. Complaints to school administrators went unheeded. Two of the faculty members facing charges moved to Israel.[25]

In far-off lands, theocrats and pedophiles seem to work well together, being one and the same in many instances. For example, in Tibet, through generations of feudal rule, young boys were snatched from their impoverished families and brought into certain monasteries to be trained as lifelong monks, domestic workers, acrobats, dance performers, and sex slaves. Tashi-Tsering, a monk, reported that he himself and numerous other peasant boys were regularly raped in the monasteries beginning at age nine.[26]

In Ghana, male fetish priests often procure girls from poor families that are said to owe an ancestral debt to the priest's forebears. The girls serve as sex slaves. The ones who manage to escape are not taken back by their fearful families. They must either return to the priest or go into town and become prostitutes.[27] In many countries, abused little girls who survive a frightful childhood are likely to become abused grown women.

A "Worldwide Plague"

Keep in mind that all the clerical child abusers taken together are but a relatively small segment of the pedophilic population. As Vatican representative Archbishop Silvano Tomasi correctly stated, "The sexual abuse of children ... is a worldwide plague and scourge."[28] Almost 30 percent of rapes in the United States involve girls eleven years or younger—and that includes only the reported cases. Another 32 percent are between eleven and seventeen. The UN's International Labor Organization reported that an estimated 10 million children worldwide, mostly from impoverished families, are forced into slavery as domestic servants in private homes, receiving no pay, no time off, no education, and no protection from sexual assault.[29] Class status is a major determinant of victimization.

China is one of the many countries in which a low visibility of pedophilia has been mistaken for its nonexistence. In May 2013, a grade school principal in Hainan Province, along with a government accomplice, raped six children. He was sentenced to 13.5 years, inciting a national outcry over the light punishment. The case and the ensuing uproar helped bring pedophilia into the open. According to a Chinese government report, an additional 125 cases were documented in 2013. Another (more realistic) report that same year listed 3,000 complaints of sexual abuse.[30] This does not necessarily signify that child rape is increasing in China. More likely, public awareness is growing; victims are coming forward and receiving firm support instead of scornful dismissal, and the Chinese government is beginning to treat the problem more seriously.

In rural villages in parts of Saudi Arabia, Pakistan, India, Bangladesh, Niger, and Nigeria, child brides, some as young as eight or nine, are married off to older men. In Iran, in 2012 alone, 1,537 girls under the age of ten and 29,827 between ten and fourteen were registered for marriage.[31] More than a million girls and boys, many as young as five or six, are conscripted into prostitution in Asia, with perhaps an equal number in the rest of the world. Pedophiles from the United States and elsewhere fuel the Asian traffic. Enjoying anonymity and impunity abroad, these "sex tourists" are inclined to treat their acts of child rape as legal and culturally acceptable.[32]

Aside from the global sex trafficking perpetrated by organized crime, child victims can be found in widely varying milieus: religious institutions, schools, team sports, day care centers, reformatories, and satanic cults.[33] At the American Boychoir School in Princeton in the 1970s and for years afterward, 30 to 40 percent of the boys were being abused: "Everyone knew and nobody did anything." Pedophilia was also prevalent at the Horace Mann School in the Bronx where a culture of sexual abuse by teachers entrenched itself; and among the Jehovah's Witnesses hierarchs who instructed elders to silence all accusations.[34]

In 2010, the Government Accountability Office (GAO) found "hundreds of potential cases of registered sex offenders working in [secular] schools" across the United States. The GAO compiled studies of 17,000 child victims. The agency also cited Department of Education studies estimating that millions of students are subjected to sexual violation during their school careers.[35]

The Boy Scouts of America has harbored pedophiles, including many Scout units sponsored by the Church of Latter-Day Saints (Mormons), with individuals who created an "infestation of child abuse, stretching across the country involving hundreds of predators and thousands of children." Meanwhile Boy Scout officials repeatedly failed to involve the police.[36] In 2012, the Boy Scouts belatedly released 14,500 pages of files revealing decades of sexual abuse, with accusations against 1,247 scout leaders, and with many instances of molestation left unreported or ignored. Many of these cases involved overt homosexual activity with underage boys. Other caches of files show repeat offenders being rotated to other Scout units, forgiven for their "misbehavior," and expected to mend their ways, much the way the Catholic Church treated its "errant priests." Parents were often kept in the dark as Boy Scout administrators showed more concern with protecting the organization's reputation than with exposing its predators.[37]

The same has been true of the scandalous cases on university campuses. A leading example is Pennsylvania State University where assistant football coach Jerry Sandusky was charged with raping at least eight boys on or near university property. He was found guilty on forty-five counts and sentenced to thirty to sixty years. Not wanting messy business to surface, some university officials originally hushed up Sandusky's exploits. They eventually were forced to resign or were fired.[38]

Just about all institutions have the same impulse to avoid public scandal and deny the existence of criminal malfeasance within their walls. To protect their institution's good name or simply to avoid costly conflicts and harm to their own careers, institutional leaders downplay even the most damaging behavior.[39] Their goal is not justice for the victims; their intent is to bury the scandal in a quiet cover-up.

Celebrity and wealth are often effective shields for predators. The late Jimmy Savile, a superstar television personality of the British Broadcasting System, was belatedly unmasked as a serial rapist of dozens of underage victims spanning a period of four decades. As of 2013, an additional 152 allegations of sexual abuse were directed at 81 current or former BBC employees.[40]

Other celebrities like Woody Allen, Roman Polanski, and J. D. Salinger are either suspected of or charged with having violated underage girls. Allen's youngest victim was Dylan Farrow who recalls being repeatedly sexually assaulted by him at the age of seven. Michael Jackson preyed upon six or more boys and spent millions in settlements with some of the victims' families.[41] Du Pont billionaire heir Robert H. Richards IV was convicted of repeatedly raping his daughter from the age of three to five as well as molesting his son starting at the age of nineteen months. But his sentence of eight years for these crimes was suspended by a sympathetic judge who thought the billionaire child rapist "would not fare well" in prison. Instead Richards was placed on an eight-year probation and ordered to attend an inpatient psychiatric program. Five years later, as of April 2014, he had yet to appear for treatment.[42]

The Family Circle

In many societies, the rapist frequently is a family member. Some years ago, in the maternity hospital of Lima, Peru, 90 percent of the young mothers ages twelve to sixteen had been raped by a father, stepfather, or another close relative.[43] The most frequent instances of child rape within the United States are to be found within the family. A psychiatric nurse, who has treated victims of incest, comments as follows:

> For every coach or babysitter or clergyman or school janitor preying on others' children, studies have shown that there are eight or nine parents, grandparents, aunts, uncles, and other relatives and their friends and significant others who molest their own children and those of their extended families.
>
> This is the dirty secret within the dirty secret of child molestation. The vast majority of it happens not in a locker room or a day camp or a ballpark but in the victim's home. The spotlight rightly shown on notorious or famous predators also serves to draw attention away from the vast majority of molesters, who are not "next door." They're in the next room.[44]

A Presbyterian minister makes a similar point: "Despite the media attention to abuse by teachers, clergymen, neighbors, and others, most abusers are believed to be family members." But to come forth with charges against a family member sometimes invites being ostracized by the entire family. Thus many survivors suffer in silence.[45] Various studies and testimonials reveal that the most common child rapes are incestuous. "There's danger in the stranger," we hear, but there is even greater danger in the manger, within the family circle where the child is most accessible, most sequestered, and most defenseless.[46]

So we see how intimate relations can be distorted by power relations, including institutions as elaborately far-reaching as the Roman Church or as immediate as the family. In an atomized, alienated society there are many opportunities to do damage to others. Poverty and patriarchy leave an open field for joint exploitation. Wealth, too, creates its own rules. Children are easy prey in a world of conniving predators. Many youngsters cannot rely on their parents. Often they have no parents, or their parents are the victimizers. We need to listen to the children and protect them from these crimes in every way possible.

8

Inequality
85 Billionaires and the Poorer Half

THROUGHOUT MOST OF THE WORLD, the super rich continue to expand the immense financial gap between themselves and the rest of us. In the face of massive inequality, they strive for still greater inequality, their goal being, in Marx's words, to "accumulate, accumulate, accumulate." Their method is to suppress the democratic struggle and liquidate the forces that strive for some modicum of economic betterment for the masses. They understand that they live off the poor, though they would rarely put it so bluntly.

An Implausible Comparison

The world's 85 richest individuals possess as much wealth as the 3.6 billion souls who compose the poorer half of the world's population, or so it was announced in a report by Oxfam International and repeated in a score of publications and broadcasts in 2014.[1] The assertion sounds implausible. The 85 richest individuals, who together are worth many thousands of billions of dollars, must have *far more* wealth than the poorest half of our global population.

How could these two cohorts, the 85 richest individuals and the 3.6 billion poorest, have the same amount of wealth? In fact, the greater portion of the 3.6 billion have no net wealth at all. Hundreds of millions of them have jobs that hardly pay enough to feed their families. Millions of them rely on supplements from private charity and public assistance when they can. Hundreds of millions suffer chronic hunger and food insecurity, including many of the very poorest in the United States. In 2012 the world's one hundred richest individuals accumulated an additional $241 billion, making them worth a total of $1.9 trillion, while close to 870 million of the world's most indigent denizens (about one in eight) endured "chronic undernourishment."[2]

Most of the impoverished 3.6 billion souls, whom we might label the "Poorer Half," earn an average of $2.50 a day. The poorest 40 percent of the world population account for just 5 percent of all global income. About 80 percent of all humanity live on less than $10 a day. And the poorest 50 percent live from hand to mouth, maintaining only 7.2 percent of the world's private consumption. How exactly could they have accumulated an amount of surplus wealth comparable to the world's 85 richest individuals?

Not only are the Poorer Half lacking in amassed wealth, many among them also have accumulated crushing debts. Hundreds of millions throughout the world live in debt. Even in a famously affluent country like the United States, more than one in three are in debt collection, that is, they have unpaid bills that are in the hands of collection agencies. They have minus zero net wealth. Millions more are on their way to falling into the hands of debt collectors.[3] Even among those Americans who are celebrated as the "middle class," we find millions who carry enormous medical debts or college tuition debts. Millions around the world are farmers and farmworkers who borrow each year hoping to reap a better crop than the year before in a continual cycle of harder toil and deeper debt. Millions have no home equity of any kind, living as they do in makeshift shacks and huts or under bridges or in old vans. In scores of countries many millions live in peonage, in what amounts to debt slavery.[4]

Of the poor in the United States who "own" homes, almost all are straddled with mortgages. "The bank is the real owner of our house," we hear people joke nervously, many of whom are not even among the very poorest in their communities. The equity that millions might have in their homes is usually far less than the size of their mortgages. Many others live "underwater," that is, they owe more on the mortgage than the house can command if it were put up for sale. This can happen if a house has declined in value during a recent recession or was sold by unscrupulous banks at a deceptively inflated price, and bought by aspiring but unpracticed homeowners. Almost 10 million households in America owe more on their mortgages than the actual market value of their homes. Unless they finally get some government intervention, they face a lifetime of paying for something that has no value except as a debt. "The blame for this tragedy," writes Peter Dreier, "lies mostly with banks' risky, reckless and sometimes illegal lending practices. . . . The federal government rescued the banks, but nobody came to the rescue of the communities the banks left behind."[5]

Those who rent apartments also face struggles. In the United States, after almost five years of serious recession, incomes remained stagnate while rents continued to rise by as much as 4 to 6 percent a year, cutting ever deeper into the budgets of modest-income households.[6]

Millions among the world's Poorer Half may have cars but many of them also have car payments. They are driving in debt. In various Third World countries, for the millions without private vehicles, there are the poorly maintained, overloaded, rickety buses that specialize in breakdowns and ravine plunges.⁷ In some parts of the world, among the lowest rungs of the impoverished are the many who pick through garbage dumps and send their kids off to work in grim, soul-destroying sweatshops or to be trafficked in sex houses or preyed upon as domestics in affluent homes.

Among the 85 richest billionaires in the world we would have to include the four members of the Walton family. As owners of Wal-Mart, they are among the top ten super rich in the United States. These fabulous four are together worth more than $100 billion. Then there are older super-rich families like the du Ponts who have controlling interests in giant corporations like General Motors and Coca-Cola. They own about forty manorial estates and private museums in Delaware alone and have set up thirty-one tax-exempt foundations.⁸ The very rich, they live differently than do we.

Next to Nothing

The Oxfam report concluded that the $110 *trillion* of wealth held by the 1 percent richest people on the planet is some sixty-five times the total wealth of those floundering about in the bottom half of the world's population pool.⁹ "In the last thirty years seven out of ten people have been living in countries where economic inequality has increased," observed Nick Galasso, one of the coauthors of the Oxfam report. "This is a trend that has been unfolding globally for the last two or three decades. What we've not seen is any political will toward curbing it."¹⁰ The report goes on: In the United States the wealthiest 1 percent have "captured 95 percent of post-financial crisis growth since 2009, while the bottom 90 percent became poorer." This ever greater concentration of economic resources in the hands of ever fewer people heightens social tensions and increases "the risk of societal breakdown." The World Economic Forum identified this enormous income inequality as one of the greatest risks facing the world today.

Regarding the poorest 50 percent of the world population—the valiant, struggling Poorer Half—what mass configuration of wealth could we possibly be talking about? Remember we are dealing with *wealth,* not income. Wealth refers to the surplus accumulation of value that is one's total material worth, not the periodical wages or salaries that are distributed for work, to be expended almost immediately on necessities. The aggregate wealth possessed by the top 85 super-rich individuals and the aggregate wealth owned by the world's 3.5 billion poorest are of different dimensions and different natures.

Can we really compare private jets, mansions, landed estates, super luxury vacation retreats, luxury apartments, luxury condos, luxury yachts, and luxury cars, not to mention hundreds of billions of dollars in equities, bonds, commercial properties, priceless art works, antiques, exquisite furnishings, jewelry, and the like—can we really compare all that enormous wealth against many millions of battered used cars, ratty furniture, and blurry television sets ready to break down? A car and a television set, along with a cow, a goat, and some chickens, can have real-use value for a poor family; but of what market resale value, if any, are such minor commodities especially in communities of widespread underemployment and subsistence wages? What surplus worth is being represented here? It seems we do not fully realize how poor the very poor really are. The number of people living in poverty is growing at a faster rate than the world's population. So poverty is spreading even as wealth expands and accumulates among the very few. It is not enough to bemoan this enormous inequality, we must also explain why it is happening. Let me repeat: The world's richest 85 individuals do not have the same amount of accumulated wealth as the world's poorest 50 percent; the top 85 filthy rich individuals have vastly *more.* The Poorer Half, the Lowest Multitude, the Great Unwashed, as they have so often been referred to, even if taken as one enormous totality, have next to nothing.

The very poor often are homeless. In America and other countries the homeless usually can procure shelter only for limited intermittent periods, if that. They face a serious problem of getting enough sleep when out on the streets. There are just so many abandoned doorways and back alleys that will shield them from both the elements and the police whose vigorous "war against crime" seems to target the most destitute and most vulnerable.[11]

Along with the shortage of money and housing—and largely because of that shortage—the poor in many countries are likely to go without decent sanitation facilities, suffering dismal health conditions and rampant diseases. Millions go through life without the benefit of any medical care. At least a billion of the poorest in the world live without toilets or even outhouses. They relieve themselves in a common openly exposed field or abandoned area. They ingest contaminated foods, suffer a lack of clean drinking water, and, as already noted, endure poor nutrition and chronic hunger.[12] Does it come as a surprise to anyone that the very poor have more disease-plagued lives and shorter life spans than people who reside in affluence?

Poor subsistence farmers throughout much of the world are committing suicide in growing numbers due to crushing debts, free trade markets, and the forced use of pesticides, terminator seeds, and chemical fertilizers. A life in poverty is a life of stress and anxiety that takes a heavy toll. In contrast, the well-to-do eat higher quality and more expensive foods; they have safer jobs, more reliable vehicles, better access to high-quality health care, better day care centers, recreation centers, retirement homes, and nursing homes, and more opportunity for self-care. Not surprisingly, they enjoy greater longevity than the less fortunate.[13]

The very poor experience a lack of advanced educational opportunities and an absence of community organization. Millions of children who number among the world's Poorer Half never see the inside of a school. They toil long days in mills, in mines, and on farms, under conditions resembling earlier centuries. Nearly a billion people are unable to read or write. By the end of the twentieth century, only a quarter of the world's children were attending school.[14]

In the supposedly rich and prosperous United States, millions of fully employed workers are not paid enough to live on. They often are referred to as the "working poor." In 2014 the US minimum wage was a paltry $7.25 an hour. Minimum wages in countries like Denmark and Switzerland were more than $20, along with more ample human services than what is provided in the United States. Full-time employees at giant American corporations like Wal-Mart, the nation's largest retailer, must supplement their poverty wages by applying for food stamps and other public assistance. Despite the growing recovery of 2013–2014, some 47 million Americans were receiving food stamps and 13 million remained out of work (not counting those who have given up looking for employment or who joined the military). No one can support a family—or oneself—on the official federal minimum wage nor on the slightly higher state minimum wages. Minimum wages are not even required to be paid to apprentices, full-time students, and workers with disabilities.[15]

Throughout the world, the Poorer Half have insufficient security of person and property, suffering great abuse at the hands of both violent criminal gangs and law enforcement authorities. The poor pay severely and repeatedly. The police serve the affluent by keeping the restive poor in line with heavy doses of harassment and violence. People of wealth do not rely solely upon corrupt and incompetent police. They also enlist private security systems in great numbers.

The very poor suffer a kind of debtor's prison. In 2013, in Ferguson, Missouri, a city of 21,135 people, the municipal court issued 32,975 arrest warrants for nonviolent offenses, mostly driving violations that people (predominantly low-income African Americans) were unable to pay. Additional fines and fees are added to and compounded with the initial charges, constituting a major source of income for the county government.[16]

The poor have far fewer opportunities to experience fairness and self-respect and other tangible and intangible conditions of life that make human existence less brutal and more bearable. Poverty imposes punishing strictures and defeats of a kind that are beyond the comprehension of the more fortunate. Poverty is not just a material condition. To millions of innocent victims, it is a situation of life that delivers constant stress and misery, both physical and psychological.

The Very Tip of the Top

As we noted in Chapter 1, the Occupy Movement directed its fire at the top 1 percent; but 1 percent of the US population consists of more than 3 million people. Most of that 1 percent make their money from salaries and commissions—rather large ones compared with what the rest of us bring home. Then there are the *very, very* rich, also known as the super rich. Derek Thompson put it well: "The rich are the same as you and I. Members of the top 1 percent make most of their money from paychecks, just like the rest of us. But the very, very rich—the 1 percent of the 1 percent—are different. They make most of their money from investments and inheritances. . . . [It is] the top 1 percent of the top 1 percent who have truly left everyone else in the dust."[17] *The top 1 percent of the top 1 percent?* Thompson is referring to the top one-hundredth of 1 percent (0.01 percent), about 30,000 individuals, dependents included: the super rich.

The top 1 percent in America, or more accurately, that fraction of 1 percent just mentioned and referred to as the super rich, own more than thirteen times as much wealth as the middle 20 percent. The top 5 percent hold more wealth than the entire remaining 95 percent of the US population.[18] Much like the bottom half of the world population, the bottom 40 percent of America's population do not even partake of wealth distribution. As already noted, on average they owe money on their mortgages, rents, unpaid taxes, credit cards, car payments, medical bills, student loans, and numerous other debts. Their net worth is below zero.[19]

Financial inequality has grown ever more steeply in recent years with the gains having gone disproportionately to the very richest among us. In just one year the four hundred most wealthy Americans pocketed $200 billion, equivalent to all the combined federal expenditures for housing, education, and food stamps. About 95 percent of the income gain that Americans have made since 2009 has gone to the top 1 percent. This same 1 percent has tripled its share of total US income.[20]

The super rich in America and in many other countries find ways, legal and illegal, to shelter much of their wealth in secret accounts. The higher one goes up the income bracket, the greater are the opportunities for enjoying tax-free income.

The richest fraction of 1 percent, that is, the top one-hundredth of 1 percent super rich, enjoy seemingly boundless tax benefits. The richer you are, the more likely your income comes from stock investments, not from salary or wages. Income from investments and inherited wealth are easier to hide than income from a paycheck. A Congressional Budget Office study revealed that, from 2002 to 2007, the growing income inequality was due to the abundance of lightly taxed or untaxed investment income.[21] The world's richest individuals have sheltered an estimated $21 trillion in offshore tax havens. At the same time, the world's biggest banks have tax sheltered an additional $10 trillion. This $31 trillion total of sheltered funds is more than the total annual gross domestic product (GDP) of the United States and Japan together.[22] Most of us really do not know how very rich the very rich really are.

Do we fully understand all that the super rich get away with? Multibillionaire Warren Buffet famously bemoaned that he paid a lower tax rate than his secretary. But favoritism for the rich is more striking than that. For instance, many Americans do not know that in any given year two of every three US companies pay no income tax. A study by the Institute on Taxation and Economic Policy showed that of 288 companies, 111 managed to pay no taxes at all.[23] You, the reader, most likely paid more income tax last year than did any number of giant corporations.

Warren Buffet also once remarked that there is a class war going on in America and his class—to his dismay—was winning. Indeed, by the beginning of 2014, corporate profits reached a record high as a share of the GDP while wages reached a new low.[24] As part of that class war, corporations control the money flow that acts so decisively upon the electoral process. They and their lobbyists are able to hone the tax laws in a way most favorable to their own interests. They accomplish this through the application of large sums of campaign funds, which guarantees that recipients write and enforce the kind of tax laws that benefit the super rich. The top 0.5 percent (top half of 1 percent) of the US population, composed largely of super-rich companies and individuals, contribute 80 percent of the campaign funds for national candidates. Elections have become the multimillionaires' game to play. Lawmakers are increasingly at the beck and call of their big-moneyed contributors.[25] The individual votes only once, if that, while the dollar votes many times.

To repeat, income inequality has grown in the United States more than ever. But *wealth* inequality also has been expanding, most dramatically at the very top of the social pyramid, among households with more than $20 million in wealth and at a still far greater rate among those who possess more than $100 million.[26] In other words, there is an ever growing inequality *within* the top 1 percent, between the rich, the middle rich, and the very super rich, with the very super rich advancing stratospherically.

Losers! Losers! Loathing the Poor

Most of the very wealthy believe that the poor are the authors of their own misery. They see the poor as given to profligacy, addiction, and wanton ways, a misfortune foisted upon us sounder citizens. The poor are lazy, incompetent, and self-indulgent, or so they appear to be in the eyes of many who occupy more favorable posts in the social pyramid.

Truth be told, the poor usually work harder for less than the rest of us. They also are more drastically exploited as homeowners and consumers. They do without what many of us would deem essential services, including health care, serviceable transportation, and decent living accommodations. With the Great Recession of 2007–2008, millions of the working poor have ended up on the unemployment rolls.

Not just in the impoverished Third World but also in the United States, continually vaunted as a prosperous nation, one finds harsh poverty and startling economic injustice. While the American plutocrats get richer and richer, *wage theft* is ever more prevalent in various parts of the country. Bosses alter time cards, fail to pay overtime rates, or refuse to pay workers at all. Even when employees manage to take legal recourse against their employer's thievery, their efforts rarely result in victory. And when they do win in court, they find it difficult to get hold of the money awarded them. Some 83 percent fail to collect. Wage theft is so prevalent in the United States as to exceed the total amount stolen in all bank, gas station, and convenience store robberies.[27]

In troubled areas around the country, most notably in blue-collar suburbs, the poor have turned to beggary. As Jennifer Medina reports about Moreno Valley, California, "The freeway exits around here are dotted with people asking for money, holding cardboard signs to tell their stories. The details vary only slightly and almost invariably include: Laid off. Need food. Young children."[28]

In supposedly rich, prosperous America, millions of the down-and-out survive only because of food stamps. But even then, they endure a serious lack of other necessities. Many families earn as much as several thousand dollars above the poverty level and thereby are not even designated as "poor" by government estimates. Yet they earn barely enough to meet their basic needs. By the time they pay for rent, gas, auto insurance, telephone, electricity, medications, and food, they are without a penny. They have no money for health insurance, dentistry, clothes, savings, child care, or further education.[29]

A survey conducted on how the top 1 percent feel about politico-economic issues does not offer an encouraging picture. It shows that the very affluent maintain little concern about economic recovery and harbor no noblesse oblige toward their less fortunate compatriots. Here are a few differences between the top 1 percent and the other 99 percent:

- Of the richest 3 million Americans (about 1 percent of the population), only 8 percent support government job creation programs and only 17 percent support heavy taxes on the rich. In contrast, more than half of the 99 percent support job programs for the needy and heavy taxes on the rich.
- About 73 percent of the richest people in America support the idea of more corporate investment overseas, while only 23 percent of everyone else is happy with that idea.
- Some 58 percent of the rich support cuts in spending on Medicare, education, and highways in order to reduce the deficit, while only 27 percent of the rest of us would follow that course.[30]

Despite their much-advertised charity balls and banquets, the super rich really do not fret much over the hardships endured by the hoi polloi—the Poorer Half—even as these hardships deepen and spread. If anything, there is often an uneasy resentment the rich feel toward the poor, especially when the latter get something for themselves, as when they collect Social Security, however inadequate it may be. The rich understand that ultimately the distribution of wealth and income does amount to a zero sum. Every dollar spent on such things as wages, occupational safety, paid vacations, health insurance, sick leave, environmental protection, and other such annoying indulgences is one less dollar pocketed by those at the apex. If everyone were prosperous there would be so much less for the top 0.01 percent. Ultimately the rich cannot be rich without the poor who labor to produce vastly more value than they are paid. The few cannot live in splendor if the many do not labor hard for them. Those at the very top understand that they have lives of preferred quality. And most of them want to keep it that way. They have a lot; they can get more; and they want it all. They understand that there is a class war going on all the time. And the only way to secure what they have accumulated is by rolling back or at least constraining whatever gains made by those of modest means. Contrary to those who talk about the community of interests between rich and poor, class struggle really *is* zero sum.[31]

Part Four

Global Rule and Ruin

9

Capitalism, a Self-Devouring Beast

THE CAPITALIST STATE PERFORMS certain essential functions long recognized by both its proponents and opponents. First, like any state, it must provide services that cannot reliably be developed through private means, such as public safety and orderly traffic, public infrastructure (roads, rails, canals, bridges, ports), and protection from natural disaster and foreign aggression. Second, there looms that most important class function of the state: securing the plutocratic interests of the very few at the top, protecting the moneyed interests from the have-nots, the 0.01 percent from the impoverished masses. The state maintains the process of capital accumulation in part by exercising methods of suppression against the working populace and its champions, using the police powers of the state, keeping the many in line in order to secure the interests of the few.

Capitalism in Chronic Contradiction

There is yet a vital third function exercised by the capitalist state, one that is seldom mentioned. It consists of using the state to prevent the capitalist system from devouring itself. Consider the core contradiction that Karl Marx pointed to: the chronic tendency toward overproduction and market crisis. An economy dedicated to speed-ups and wage cuts, making workers produce more and more goods and services for relatively less and less recompense, is always in danger of crashing in upon itself. Recessions occur when workers are not paid enough to buy back the goods and services they produce. Capitalism constantly tends toward overcapacity, producing too many goods and services that too few consumers can afford to buy, resulting in market crises, crashes, recessions, and panics.

To maximize profits, which is the one great goal of all capitalist production, wages must be kept down. For the capitalists, every dollar spent on such bothersome things as wages, benefits, occupational safety, and environmental protections is one less dollar in profits. So the capitalist does everything possible to keep wages and other production costs as low as possible.

But someone has to buy the goods and services being produced. For that, wages need to be kept up. As an owner I would want to pay my workers as little as possible. At the same time I would want other owners to pay their workers enough so they can buy the goods and services that my workers produce. But other owners have the same idea, the same self-serving commitment to keeping labor costs down—both by paying workers less and by employing fewer workers. So there exists a chronic tendency toward overproduction of private sector commodities and services (and underconsumption of much-needed services supplied by the public sector). The contradictory pressure within the entire system is to maximize production while minimizing the disposable income of the workforce. It is as if the capitalists were striving to undo their own system.

Economic crises are not exceptional; they are a familiar condition of the corporate capitalist system. The abnormal is the norm. Consider US free market history. After the American Revolution, there were the debtor rebellions of the late 1780s, the panic of 1792, the recession of 1809 (lasting several years), the panics of 1819 and 1837, and recessions and crashes through much of the rest of that century. The serious recession of 1893 continued for more than a decade.

How does the capitalist state address this problem? Theodore Roosevelt found a solution: "I should welcome almost any war, for I think this country needs one."[1] A war brings the economic stimulus that comes with enormous increases in government spending. War wins access to colonies rich in resources. War also distracts the public from its domestic grievances. Urged onward by political leaders and opinion molders, underemployed citizens rally around the flag and fight for the empire, all the while thinking of themselves as liberators of some sort. Civilians would find employment in munitions plants or enlistment in the army or navy. In Roosevelt's day, a war certainly did come—against Spain, much to the satisfaction of McKinley, Roosevelt, and others of their class.[2] Then came the industrial recession of 1900–1915, with the panic of 1907 (engineered by J. P. Morgan), succeeded by the agrarian depression of the 1920s—cloaked behind the razzle-dazzle of the Jazz Age and the Roaring Twenties.

All this was followed by the unforgettable crash of the Great Depression of 1929, which continued up until the United States entered World War II in December 1941.[3] Through much of the twentieth century we had wars, cold wars, recessions, inflation, boom-and-bust cycles, labor struggles, and chronic underemployment. Wars and recessions help to increase capital concentration; they help big capital to monopolize labor markets and consumer markets; they plunder natural resources and weaken worker resistance toward management. The brutish vagaries of plutocracy and the hyperbolic outpouring of patriotism are not the products of particular personalities but of systemic interests.

Our White House leaders come from different regions, different families, schools, churches, and social backgrounds. They have different personalities, yet they pursue pretty much the same policies on behalf of the same configuration of powerful systemic interests. I am not arguing that all policy decisions are firmly fixed. Unintended consequences, troublesome personalities, and other unexpected oddities do arise in the realm of public policy and worldly affairs, as in personal life itself. But we also must take account of interest-driven intentions. More often than not, the "aberrations"—be they wars, market crashes, famines, or whatever—take shape because those at the top are pursuing gainful acquisitions. Knowing your class opponents and what they are capable of doing is the first step toward effective opposition. Only then does the world become less of a horrific puzzlement. We can only resist these global (and local) perpetrators when we see who they are and what they are continually doing to us and our priceless environment.

Saving Capitalism from the Capitalists

During the 1990s in Argentina, we witnessed the collapse of an entire economy. Unrestrained free marketeers stripped whole corporations, pocketed vast sums, and left the country's productive capacity in shambles. Having gorged on a heavy diet of free market ideology, the Argentine plutocrats faltered in the third function of the state: saving capitalism from the capitalists.[4]

Some years later, during the George W. Bush administration in the United States, there came the multibillion-dollar plunder perpetrated by corporate conspirators at Enron, WorldCom, Harkin, Adelphia, and a dozen other major companies.[5] Inside players (like White House crony Ken Lay) turned successful and prosperous corporate enterprises into wreckage, wiping out the jobs and life savings of thousands of their own employees in order to pocket ill-begotten fortunes for themselves. Nor should it seem strange that capitalists would loot their own ventures. Their consuming loyalty is not to the capitalist system as such but to their personal fortunes.

That some of these thieves were caught and convicted does not mean that capitalism has an automatic self-correcting free market mechanism. The prosecution of malfeasance—in the rare occasions it happens—is a product of *democracy's* accountability and transparency, not capitalism's. In the Enron case and others of that day, it was the state, the public authority, that prosecuted the scoundrels. Of itself the free market is an amoral system, with no moral strictures save *caveat emptor.*

With the recession meltdown of 2007–2008, the mounting financial surplus posed a problem for the moneyed class: There were not enough opportunities for gainful investment. Possessing more money than they knew what to do with, big investors poured immense sums into multibillion-dollar, nonexistent housing markets and such dodgy connivances as hedge funds, derivatives, high leveraging, credit default swaps, and predatory lending. Among the victims of the corporate investors were other (smaller) investors and the many employees who lost billions in savings and pensions. Yet no one went to jail in 2008 or thereafter. One dramatic exception was the filching brigand Bernard Madoff, who was unconnected to any large corporation and who stole from the rich all on his own. Described as "a longstanding leader in the financial services industry," Madoff ran a Ponzi scheme that grossed $50 billion from wealthy investors, paying them back "with money that wasn't there," as he himself playfully put it. He was convicted and sentenced to 150 years in prison in 2009, a big-time swindler made to do big time in the Big House.[6]

In the midst of the Great Recession meltdown, at an October 2008 congressional hearing, former chair of the Federal Reserve and free market devotee Alan Greenspan, in an unconvincing display of innocence, confessed that he had been foolish to expect that moneyed interests would suddenly exercise self-restraint and self-regulation.[7] The big-moneyed interests were incapable of regulating themselves in any orderly fashion, Greenspan admitted.

The classic laissez-faire theory is even more preposterous than Greenspan makes it. The theory claims that everyone *should* pursue their own selfish interests and do so without restraint or regulation. This unbridled competition supposedly would produce maximum benefits for all because the free market is governed by a miraculously benign "invisible hand" that optimizes collective outputs. "Greed is good."

Truth be told, capitalism has no commitment to mutual betterment and communal refinement. "One capitalist always kills many," Marx wrote bluntly; competition leads to an "expropriation of many capitalists by few."[8] The goal of any corporation, he was saying, is to outdo and eventually eliminate corporate competitors.

The promoters of "free enterprise" regularly pay homage to competition. It is competition that brings out the best in us, stoking our determination and inventiveness, so we hear. In fact, the corporate oligarchs form informal trusts when they can; they fix prices and try to monopolize access to essential resources; they misrepresent their products to consumers and underpay their workers as much as possible, all to advantage themselves against competitors. From the meatpacking industry to the auto industry, numerous smaller producers were driven out and only a few giant firms remained standing. Capitalists do everything they can to undercut their competitors. They hate competition even as they sing its praises.

Big capital does not necessarily dislike recessions. Large companies more easily crush small competitors and not-so-small competitors. In time, giant firms ingest other giant firms so that only a select few remain standing. Competition pushes toward monopoly. The plutocracy devours its children. Meanwhile, with shutdowns and increased unemployment, labor unions suffer drastically weakened bargaining positions. The only thing that sometimes protects the capitalist system from itself is the rigorous regulations of capitalist government. But the government is seldom up to the regulatory task. The state cannot easily discipline those whom it serves.

Unscrupulous Individuals or Disastrous System?

Is the self-destruction and chronic instability of the corporate profit-driven system a product of greedy scoundrels, or is it inherent in the competitive system itself? Was the crisis of 2007–2008 caused by a chronic tendency toward overproduction and hyper-financial accumulation, as Marx might have it? Or was it the outcome of the personal avarice of people like Bernard Madoff? In other words, is the crisis systemic or individual? Is the system created by scoundrels, or does it itself create scoundrels? In fact, the two are not mutually exclusive. Capitalism breeds the venal perpetrators and rewards the most unscrupulous among them. And they, in turn, do the system's dirty work.

Let us keep in mind that the economic crimes and crises are not irrational departures from a rational capitalist system, but the converse: They are the rational (inevitable) outcomes produced by an avaricious, irrational system. Worse still, the ensuing multibillion-dollar government bailouts are themselves turned into an opportunity for pillage. Not only does the state fail to regulate sufficiently, it itself becomes a major source of plunder, pulling vast sums from the federal money machine while leaving the taxpayers to bleed.

Those reactionaries who scold us for "running to the government for handouts" are themselves constantly running to the government for handouts. Corporate America has always enjoyed grants-in-aid, loan guarantees, massive subsidies, shameless tax write-offs, and other state and federal subventions. But the 2007–2008 "rescue operation" offered corporate America a record feed at the public trough. More than $350 billion was dished out by a right-wing lame-duck secretary of the treasury, Henry Paulson, to the biggest banks and financial houses without any oversight—not to mention the more than $4 trillion that came from the Federal Reserve. Most of the banks, including JPMorgan Chase and Bank of New York Mellon, stated that they had no intention of letting anyone know where the Fed's money was going.[9]

We do know that the "too-big-to-fail" banks used some of the bailout to buy up smaller banks and prop up their own overseas franchises. Top banking executives spent bailout funds on fabulous bonuses and lavish corporate spa retreats. Meanwhile, big bailout beneficiaries like Citigroup and Bank of America laid off tens of thousands of employees. While huge sums of money were being doled out to the very people who had caused the catastrophe, the housing market continued to wilt, credit remained paralyzed, unemployment worsened, and consumer spending sank to record lows.

Belatedly in 2013–2014, major financial institutions, including Bank of America, Goldman Sachs, Wells Fargo, J.P. Morgan Chase, and Citigroup agreed to pay many billions of dollars for federal and state lawsuit claims regarding mortgage securities. In 2014 other financial institutions such as Credit Suisse pleaded guilty to aiding tax evasion and agreed to pay $2.6 billion to settle a long-running probe by the US Justice Department. Also in 2014 a French bank, BNP Paribas, agreed to pay nearly $9 billion to the US government and pleaded guilty to concealing prohibited transactions. Despite these large penalties, in none of these cases were any perpetrators incarcerated.[10] Their banks were too big to fail and their executives too big to jail.

The essence of free market corporate capitalism is the transformation of living nature into mountains of fabricated commodities and the transformation of commodities into heaps of dead capital. When left entirely to its own devices, capitalism foists its diseconomies and toxicity upon the general public and upon the natural environment. At the same time it continues to devour itself so that a small cluster of pathological profiteers may pocket more and more in pursuit of eternal self-enrichment.

The immense economic inequality that exists in our capitalist society translates into a formidable inequality of political power, which makes it all the more difficult to impose democratic regulations and restrictions. If the paladins of corporate America want to know what really threatens "our way of life," it is *their* way of life—their boundless pilfering of their own system, destroying the very foundation upon which they stand, the very community upon which they so lavishly feed.

The Great American Prosperity

We are taught that capitalism is a system that works, a system that has created immense prosperity, most strikingly in the United States. But in the previous chapter we discussed the poverty and hardship suffered by millions of Americans and the many millions who inhabit other countries. We saw that capitalist prosperity is highly selective and grows increasingly unequal and top-heavy.

The much-celebrated American prosperity was actually confined to a period that lasted not much longer than four decades, from about 1946 to the early 1980s. In the years before World War II, during the Great Depression, the Franklin Roosevelt administration with its New Deal produced some long-overdue social welfare legislation, including retirement pensions, disability insurance, and survivors insurance (for children of deceased workers), all part of Social Security as we know it today. The New Deal created a number of worthwhile conservation and public works projects, a rural electrification program, and a reduction in unemployment from 25 percent to 19 percent. Millions of hungry and destitute people were fed and sheltered. The New Deal built or improved roads across the country and constructed schools, parks, playgrounds, athletic fields, and airports, along with hospitals, post offices, bridges, tunnels, and courthouses. It created thousands of acres of campgrounds and improvements in firefighting, rodent control, water conservation, and prevention of soil erosion. The New Deal also passed a number of key laws that strengthened the bargaining rights of labor unions.[11]

Still the common people were ready to go further than Roosevelt did. They probably would have accepted a nationalized banking system, a national health-care system, and most certainly a more massive job program. The New Deal did many good things, but it never lifted the national economy out of the Great Depression.

Then came World War II, a blood-drenched success story. The gross national product, which stood at $88 billion in 1940, mushroomed to $135 billion within a few years of the US entry into the war. At the same time, manufacturing output more than doubled. Those who profited most were the industrial tycoons and arms contractors. But some of the big spending did trickle down. Almost all of the 8.7 million unemployed were either drafted into the armed forces or drawn into the industrial workforce, along with 10 million new workers. Of these latter, some 6 million were woman who now found jobs in shipyards, lumber mills, steel mills, and defense plants. There were female welders, riveters, electricians, and mechanics. Women operated streetcars, buses, cranes, and tractors. Female engineers and scientists were now able to find work in leading industrial laboratories. And women ran farms, tended animals, and harvested tons of vegetables, fruits, and grains.[12]

Many people were now earning wages substantially higher than anything available during Depression days. Only by entering the war and remaining thereafter in a state of permanent war economy was the country able to significantly reduce unemployment. The same plutocracy that was incapable of making an all-out spending effort to feed and house people in peacetime was able to make an all-out effort to kill people in wartime.

Many citizens feared that once World War II ended, the government would make massive cutbacks in spending: Ten million young men would come pouring back into the civilian sector looking for jobs, and once again the nation would collapse into a monumental depression. But things went in a different direction.

First: Much of the civilian population made fairly good money during the war years, certainly better than during the Great Depression. But there was relatively little to spend it on. The auto and appliance factories were too busy making tanks, ships, and planes. Other facilities produced food, clothing, and medical care for the millions in the armed forces, while the civilian population was subjected to food and fuel rationing. After the war there was an unprecedented backlog of buying power and consumer demand of a kind only dreamed of during the Depression. In addition, most women employees were pushed back into their homes, making room on the job market for returning veterans.

Second: Millions of veterans, who might otherwise have been looking for work, took advantage of the educational opportunities offered by the federal government's GI Bill.[13] Publications like the Hearst newspapers reprinted old photos of veterans selling apples on street corners after World War I, accompanied with captions like "Never again." This time returning veterans were to get better treatment. Millions of them received professional and vocational training with free tuition and full stipends. Here was an educational undertaking like nothing before in American history, one that also provided a substantial upgrading to the economy. (The original GI Bill was unlike the GI Bill of today with its insufficient funding. Today's recipients usually need to work one or two part-time jobs and take out student loans in order to survive.)

Third: There came the Cold War, which ultimately lasted five decades. Military spending once more became a huge yearly stimulus package, as it had been during the war and as it so remains now in these days of global empire. Pentagon Keynesianism, as some called it, from the postwar era to this day has been a source of enormous profit for corporate America, well-paying jobs for a segment of the workforce, and astronomical deficits for the US taxpayers.

Fourth: In 1945 and for decades thereafter, Red Army troops were situated on the Elba. In France and Italy there emerged large, well-organized communist parties. Eastern European countries were ruled by communists; whatever their problems and abuses, their populations did have subsidized housing, free education to the highest levels, a guaranteed right to a job, socialized health care, and free (or very affordable) utilities, museums, concerts, and sporting events. The Western capitalists, facing serious labor struggles and concerned that their own working classes might hanker for a socialistic agenda, reluctantly made some substantial concessions. They grudgingly showed a friendlier regard toward industrial unions and agreed to minimum wages, company health insurance, and most New Deal programs.

By the 1950s America was moving from the Dust Bowl poverty of the Great Depression to the comforts of suburbia, a world where inhabitants could buy (in installments) automobiles, appliances, and even homes. A majority could expect a living wage with modest income increases, no massive debt, and affordable college education at state and municipal universities for their children.[14] Here indeed was a *middle class* for people who earlier had only dreamed of such things. With it came the constant blather about America as a land of prosperity and golden opportunity where each generation would live a still better life than the one before.

When Capitalism Creates Poverty

Prosperity comes in capitalist society when democratic forces are finally able to extract class gains from an owning class that is usually prepared to yield nothing. Consider northern European countries like Sweden, Finland, Denmark, Norway, and a few others. In such lands, well-organized leftist parliamentary parties with strong support from organized labor were able to win important gains and construct viable *social democracies,* as they are called. Social democracies are countries that have many of the securities and services that the full-blown socialist countries in Eastern Europe once had, while retaining a privatized economic sector along with parliamentary democracy, civil liberties, and organized dissent.

But what has capitalism delivered elsewhere? Almost the entire world is capitalist and almost the entire world is raggedly poor. There is capitalist Indonesia; it is miserably poor and getting poorer. So with capitalist India, Thailand, Nigeria, Liberia, El Salvador, Haiti, Mexico, South Africa, Honduras, El Salvador, Poland, and Ukraine—all capitalist and all in the grip of "free trade," privatization, heavy indebtedness, and cutbacks in their already meager human services. Capitalism does not work well at all for the people in those countries. It brings not prosperity but hardship. As capitalism spreads, so does the poverty it creates.

We usually do not think of Third World countries as being capitalist. In fact, Third World poverty is capitalism at its most successful. Capitalism in countries like Indonesia, Colombia, and Nigeria works quite well for the capitalists, unlike capitalism in, say, Norway and Finland where the plutocrats must deal with heavy taxes on the rich, well-funded human services for the general public, and strong environmental protections. In the Third World, the capitalist plutocracy has its way with just about everything, paying starvation wages, enjoying easy access to precious resources, piling up big profits, and answerable to no one.

Let us accept the idea that, compared with the Third World, many of us Americans live in material abundance. However, it was not capitalism that gave us this standard of living; it was the democratic struggle *against* capitalism. Why don't we Americans work for fifteen cents an hour, as unfortunates do in certain other countries—and as we did in 1900? Is it because we have become so much more self-respecting? More likely it is because the democratic class struggle over the generations in the United States advanced to a more favorable historical level, allowing citizens to demand better wages and conditions, unlike the brutal colonization and repression perpetrated in the Third World by the transnational corporate empire builders.[15] All through the nineteenth and early twentieth centuries, America was a Third World country—decades before the term had been coined.

The term *Third World* gained currency during the Cold War era. The United States and the Western capitalist nations were considered the First World. The Soviet bloc countries were designated the Second World. And the deeply impoverished countries of Asia, Africa, and Latin America were labeled the Third World. I prefer "Third World" to "developing nations" because the Third World nations—under the heel of global capitalism—have not been developing in any way that might be considered beneficial to their peoples.

In the early part of the twentieth century, millions of Americans were still ill-housed and ill-fed. Underemployment, low wages, and merciless long work hours were commonplace. Millions of children went without schooling or adequate nourishment, and child labor was widespread. There were no social services other than a few soup kitchens and charities. There were typhoid epidemics in our major cities, along with tuberculosis and other diseases of poverty.

That is what capitalism gave us: an unregulated free market, complete with massive fortunes for the Mellons and Morgans, the Rockefellers and du Ponts, and the Carnegies and Vanderbilts. But the plutocrat's fear was (and still is) that egalitarian efforts by the masses ultimately lead to a class leveling that might jeopardize the system of self-enrichment for the few. Instead of free market capitalism, we might end up with a social democracy—or worse.

Advances in our living standards were not a gift from the plutocracy; they were the achievements of working people and other socially conscious individuals who thought that a society should be governed by something better than profit pathologies. So they fought for the eight-hour day and five-day workweek, for public education and health services, public transportation, decent housing, a livable minimum wage, a progressive income tax, Social Security, Medicare, Medicaid, occupational safety, and environmental protections. And it has been the "economic royalists," as Franklin Roosevelt called them back during the New Deal, who have resisted just about every egalitarian effort. Every modicum of prosperity we achieved was won against their will.

The Rollback

Further gains in social services were won through the 1960s and into the mid-1970s. Social Security was proving itself to be the most successful antipoverty program in the country's history, at the same time piling up billion-dollar surpluses (even as reactionaries continued to predict its insolvency). Then came Medicare in 1966. Occupational safety, consumer safety, and environmental protections became part of state and federal social services. Recessions still occurred now and then, but it was regarded as an age of prosperity in a land of widely distributed wealth, a prosperity mistakenly characterized as the longstanding, God-given condition of life in America. Even in this relatively prosperous period, there was that "other America," the one inhabited by tens of millions of people who lived below or barely above the poverty line where life was burdened by heavy deprivations.[16]

It seemed that the United States was indeed becoming a social democracy, a land of government handouts to welfare chiselers, as many reactionary political leaders put it. In 1971, future Supreme Court Justice Lewis F. Powell Jr. urged, in a memorandum to the chair of the

Chamber of Commerce's education committee, a long-range campaign to make free enterprise and conservatism the dominant viewpoint in America. Needed most was an ideological struggle to roll back the liberal dominance and bring forth conservative supremacy in the media, academia, secondary schools, the political arena, and the world of ideas in general. "Powell's then seemingly improbable plan has been fully realized," James Tracy reminds us.[17]

A few years before Powell's memorandum, the "long march through institutions" was hailed as a way to state power, a strategy of the 1960s radicals. But instead it was the reactionaries who made the long march with their well-financed think tanks, law schools, institutions of "higher earning," academic graduate schools, and mass media outlets, buying up or financing publications, scholarly research, radio talk shows, and whole propaganda networks such as FOX News. Meanwhile the "liberal media," with its timorous centrist stance, has been misleadingly treated as a left equivalent to the extreme rightists on the air. So with the corporate radio stations. But in fact the right-wing talk-show hosts vastly outstrip the liberal ones both in number of outlets and ideological range. The conservatives have waged a successful ideological campaign for several decades, while the liberals trembled in a corner, acting like the battered spouse in an abusive relationship.

Earlier I noted the nation's mass inequalities, the tens of millions of people who struggle from hand to mouth, the many millions who live without a trace of economic security. Then there are the desperate ones at the very bottom. About one in every five people in the United States chronically suffers from food insecurity. Millions face regressive taxes, overwork, loss of benefits, lifetime debts, the defunding of public sector services, and the deterioration of a once livable environment. The reactionary's goal is to get the United States back to 1900: a world with a poor working class and a shrunken middle class ruled over by a privileged coterie possessed of astronomical fortune. This rollback has been on its way for a number of years and is getting worse with time.

10

Profit Pathology and Disposable Planet

SOME YEARS AGO IN NEW ENGLAND, a group of environmentalists asked a corporate executive how his company (a paper mill) could justify dumping its raw industrial effluent into a nearby river. The river—which had taken Mother Nature hundreds of centuries to create—had been used for drinking water, fishing, boating, and swimming. But in just a few years, the paper mill turned it into a highly toxic open sewer. The executive shrugged and said that river dumping was the most cost-effective way of removing the mill's wastes. If the company had to absorb the additional expense of having to clean up after itself, it might not be able to maintain its competitive edge and would then have to go out of business or move to a cheaper labor market, resulting in a loss of jobs for the local economy.

Free Market Über Alles

It was a familiar argument: The company had no choice. It was compelled to act that way in a competitive free market. Such are the blessings of competition. The mill was not in the business of protecting the environment but in the business of making a profit, the highest possible profit. The overriding purpose of private enterprise is capital accumulation. As business leaders make clear when pressed on the point, profit is the name of the game.

We have been asked to believe that in the paradise of laissez-faire capitalism, the most avaricious individuals, in pursuit of the most irresponsible self-serving ends, can ride bronco across a wide-open free market, unbridled and unrestrained, while miraculously producing optimal outcomes beneficial for all of society. Tell it to the miserable victims of world poverty.

The pursuit of wealth is a dangerous and costly addiction. Capitalist societies, by definition, are dedicated to such a pursuit and are furiously addicted. The free marketeers have a deep all-abiding faith in laissez-faire. It is a faith that serves them well. It allows no government oversight and no accountability for the environmental disasters they perpetrate. At the same time, like glutinous gourmands, the captains of industry and finance forget their free market cant and repeatedly get themselves bailed out by the government, the very same government they denounce for lending assistance to other less greedy but more needy working people. Thus fortified, corporate heads can continue to take irresponsible risks, plunder the land, poison the water, sicken whole communities, lay waste to entire regions, and pocket high profits.

This corporate system of capital accumulation treats the planet's life-sustaining resources (arable land, drinkable groundwater, viable wetlands, forests, fisheries, ocean beds, bays, rivers, clean air) as disposable ingredients presumed to be of limitless supply, to be consumed or toxified at will. As BP (the multinational oil company) demonstrated in the 2010 catastrophic oil spill in the Gulf of Mexico, considerations of cost weigh so much more heavily than considerations of safety and precaution. One congressional inquiry concluded, "Time after time, it appears that BP made decisions that increased the risk of a blowout to save the company time or expense."[1]

Indeed, the purpose of the transnational corporation is not to promote a healthy ecology but to extract as much market value out of the natural world as possible, even if it means treating the environment like a septic tank. An ever-expanding corporate capitalism and a fragile finite ecology are on a calamitous collision course, so much so that the support systems of the entire ecosphere—the Earth's thin skin of fresh air, clean water, and topsoil—are seriously at risk. It is not true that the ruling interests are in a state of denial about all this. Worse than denial, they have shown outspoken antagonism toward those who think our planet is more important than their profiteering. So they defame environmentalists as eco-terrorists, EPA Gestapo, Earth Day alarmists, tree huggers, and purveyors of Green hysteria.[2]

Most of the diseconomies of big business are foisted upon the general populace, including the costs of cleaning up toxic wastes, the cost of monitoring production and environmental impact, the cost of disposing of industrial effluence (which composes 40 to 60 percent of the loads treated by taxpayer-supported municipal sewerage plants), the cost of developing new water sources (while industry and agribusiness consume 80 percent of the nation's daily water supply not including the immense amounts destroyed by fracking), and the costs of attending to the sickness caused by all the toxicity created. With many of these diseconomies regularly passed on to the government, the private sector then boasts of its superior cost-efficiency over the public sector.

The Super Rich Are Different from Us

Isn't ecological disaster a threat to the health and survival of plutocrats just as it is a threat to us ordinary citizens? We can understand why the corporate rich might want to destroy public housing, public education, government postal service, Social Security, Medicare, and Medicaid. Such cutbacks would bring us closer to a free market society devoid of the publicly funded "socialistic" human services that the reactionaries detest. And such cuts would not deprive the super rich and their families of anything. They have more than sufficient wealth to procure whatever *private* services and protections they need for themselves.

There already are a number of public services that have been deprived of government support and thrown to the tender mercies of the free market. For instance, guaranteed paid maternity leave for new mothers. In a country like the United States, supposedly so prosperous and so constantly hailing "family values," one would think that new mothers would be given some paid leave from their jobs. In England, new mothers receive paid maternity leave for 280 work days, in Russia 140 days, in China 90 days, and even in Saudi Arabia 70 days. But in the United States it is *zero* days of paid maternity leave for new mothers.[3] (Some other deficiencies in US medical services have been touched upon earlier in Chapters 5 and 6.)

The US plutocrats seek to roll back human services. We might invite them to take pride in the fact that the United States is "Number One" in such unregulated things as total crimes, incarceration rates, CO_2 emissions, divorce rates, heart attacks, and unlabeled genetically modified food products (outlawed in more than thirty other countries).[4]

But the environment is a story different from public services, is it not? Do not wealthy reactionaries and their corporate lobbyists inhabit the same polluted planet as everyone else? Do they not eat the same chemicalized food and breathe the same toxified air? In fact, they do not live exactly as everyone else. They experience a different class reality, often residing in places where the air is markedly better than in low- and middle-income areas. They have access to food that is organically raised and specially transported and prepared. The nation's toxic dumps and freeways usually are not situated in or near their swanky neighborhoods. In fact, the super rich usually do not live in neighborhoods as such. They are likely to reside on landed estates with plenty of wooded areas, streams, meadows, and only a few well-monitored access roads. Pesticide sprays are not poured over their trees and gardens. Clear cutting does not desolate their ranches, estates, family forests, hillsides, lakes, and prime vacation spots.

Still, shouldn't they fear the threat of an ecological apocalypse brought on by global warming, with its massive and multiple fires and hurricanes, tornadoes and earthquakes, the nuclear plant disasters and merciless droughts, the die-offs of porpoises, bees, and other species? Do the very rich want to see life on Earth, including their own lives, destroyed? In the long run they indeed will be sealing their own doom along with everyone else's. However, like us all, they live not in the long run but in the here and now. What is now at stake for them is something more proximate and more urgent than global ecology; it is global profits. The fate of the biosphere seems like a remote abstraction compared with the fate of one's immediate—and enormous—investments.

With their eye on the bottom line, big-business leaders know that every dollar a company spends on environmental protection is one less dollar to be pocketed. Moving away from fossil fuels and toward solar, wind, and tidal energy could help avert ecological disaster, but six of the world's ten top industrial corporations are involved primarily in the production of oil, gasoline, and gas-guzzling motor vehicles.

Fossil fuel pollution brings billions of dollars in returns. Ecologically sustainable forms of production threaten to compromise such profits, the big producers are convinced.

Immediate gain for oneself is a far more compelling consideration than a future loss shared by the general public. Every time you drive your car, you are putting your immediate need to get somewhere ahead of the collective and seemingly remote need to avoid poisoning the air we breathe. So with the big players: The social cost of turning a forest into a wasteland weighs little against the immediate profit that comes from harvesting the timber. And then come the handy rationalizations: There are lots of other forests for people to visit; they don't need this one. Consumers need the timber, lumberjacks need the jobs, and so on.

The Future Is Now

Some of the very same scientists and environmentalists who see the ecological crisis as urgent rather annoyingly warn us of a catastrophic climate crisis by "the end of this century." But that is decades away when most of us and even most of our children will be dead—which makes global warming a much less urgent issue. Most of us live in the here and now, not in the end of the century.

There are other scientists who manage to be even more irritating by warning us of an impending ecological crisis then putting it even further into the future: "We'll have to stop thinking in terms of eons and start thinking in terms of centuries," one scientific sage was quoted in the *New York Times* in 2006. This is supposed to put us on alert? If a global catastrophe is several centuries away, who is going to make the terribly difficult and costly decisions today on behalf of distant unborn generations?

Often we are told to think of our dear grandchildren who will be fully victimized by it all (an appeal usually made in a mournful and beseeching tone). But most of the young people I address on college campuses have a hard time imagining the world that their nonexistent grandchildren will be experiencing some fifty years hence.

Such appeals should be put to rest. We do not have centuries or generations or even many decades before disaster is upon us. Ecological crisis is not some distant challenge. Most of us alive today probably will not have the luxury of saying *Après moi, le déluge* because we will still be around to experience the catastrophe ourselves. We know this to be true because the ecological crisis is already acting upon us with an accelerated and compounded effect that may soon prove irreversible.

The Profiteering Pathology

Sad to say, the environment cannot defend itself. It is up to us to protect it—or what's left of it. But the oligarchs want to keep transforming living nature into dead capital. Impending ecological disasters are of no great moment to the corporate plunderers. Of living nature they have no measure.

Wealth becomes addictive. Its accumulation becomes an all-consuming passion. Fortune whets the appetite for still more fortune. There is no end to the amount of money the super rich might wish to accumulate. So the accumulation addicts gather more and more for themselves, more than can be spent in a thousand lifetimes of limitless indulgence, driven by what begins to resemble an obsessional pathology, a monomania that blots out other human considerations.

So the plutocrats—with their enormous fortunes, elite education, lavish lives, and global contacts—convince themselves that they are God's gift to humanity. They live amid the finer things of life, which of itself makes them feel they are the finer people. They are more wedded to their wealth than to the Earth upon which they live, more concerned about the fate of their fortunes than the fate of humanity, so possessed by their pursuit of profit as to not see the disaster looming ahead.

There was a *New Yorker* cartoon showing a corporate executive standing at a lectern addressing a business meeting with these words: "And so, while the end-of-the-world scenario will be rife with unimaginable horrors, we believe that the pre-end period will be filled with unprecedented opportunities for profit."[5] Not such a joke. Years ago I remarked that those who denied the existence of global warming would not change their opinion until the North Pole itself started melting. (I never expected it to actually start dissolving in my lifetime.) Today we are facing an Arctic meltdown that carries horrendous implications for the oceanic gulf streams, coastal water levels, the planet's entire temperate zone, and world agricultural output.

So how are the captains of industry and finance responding? As we might expect: like monomaniacal profiteers. They hear only the music of gold coins jingling in their pockets. *First,* they tell us, the Arctic melting will open a direct northwest passage between the two great oceans, a dream older than Lewis and Clark. This will make for shorter and more accessible and inexpensive global trade routes. No more having to plod through the Panama Canal or around Cape Horn. Lower transportation costs means more trade and higher profits.

Second, they joyfully note that the melting is opening up vast new oil reserves to drilling. They will be able to "drill-baby-drill" for more of the same fossil fuel that is causing the very calamity descending upon us. More meltdown means more oil and more profits; such is the mantra of the free marketeers who think the world belongs only to them. Listen to the rhapsodizing of one of the presumably less reactionary proponents of global capitalism, erstwhile US Secretary of State Hillary Clinton: "The melting of sea ice ... will result in more shipping, fishing and tourism, and the possibility to develop newly accessible oil and gas reserves. We seek to pursue these opportunities in a smart, sustainable way that preserves the Arctic environment and ecosystem."[6] How exactly do they preserve and sustain an ecosystem they are drastically disfiguring and destroying? Clinton did not say.

When Socialism Works Better Than Capitalism

Many Americans have been taught to place their faith in the free enterprise system. The ideological drumbeat goes on and on, dominated by the corporate media's reactionary outpourings. The right-wing opinion molders understand that words and (dis)information—properly honed and repeatedly transmitted—can create images and ideas that get riveted into our heads. Words and declamations shape thoughts. Thoughts shape beliefs. And beliefs generate and interpret actions.

Against all contrary preachment and fixed ideology, I find myself advocating socialism over capitalism because in most areas of vital production socialism works so much better than profit-obsessed capitalism. Socialism serves human need rather than human greed. But can the government really produce anything of worth? For a response to that question, one might ask corporate America itself. In fact, a number of private industries exist today only because the government funded the research and development and provided most or all the risk capital, for instance railroads, satellite communication, aeronautics, the Internet, and nuclear power.

The entire defense industry and Pentagon arsenal is publicly funded and directed. (Again, we have trillions in public funds for killing people but not enough for housing and feeding people.) Market forces are not a necessary basis for scientific and technological development. The great achievements of numerous US university and government laboratories during and after World War II were conducted under conditions of central federal planning and public funding.

Our roads and some utilities are publicly owned, as are our bridges, ports, and airports. In some states so are liquor stores, which yearly generate hundreds of millions of dollars in state revenues. There are credit unions and a few privately owned banks like the Community Bank of the Bay (Northern California) whose primary purpose is to make loans to low- and middle-income communities. We need public banks that can be capitalized with state funds and with labor union pensions that are now in private banks. The Bank of North Dakota is the only bank wholly owned by a state. In earlier times it helped farmers who were being taken advantage of by grain monopolies and private banks. Today, the Bank of North Dakota is an important source of credit for farmers, small businesses, and local governments.[7] It is no accident that North Dakota is one of only two states that have not been drowning in debt and deficits in recent years. Other states have considered creating state banks, but private banking interests with their lobbyists and big campaign contributions have been able to block enactment.

We should create a national bank with money issued directly by the Treasury Department to provide low-interest, easy-term loans for people who want to start small businesses, go to school, or own a home—a national bank that is run on a nonprofit basis, the goal being not to plunder the public on behalf of big banks but to make credit available for those who have a productive need.

Today's United States harbors more than 30,000 worker-owned producer cooperatives and thousands of consumer cooperatives, along with credit unions, housing co-ops, rural utility co-ops, cooperative banks, cooperative insurance companies, and telecommunication and cable co-ops. Employees own a majority of the stock in at least a thousand companies.[8] Construction trade unions have used pension funds to build low-cost housing and to start unionized, employee-owned contracting firms. The Organic Consumers Association, with a membership of 250,000 strong, works for the conversion of the nation's agricultural system to organic farming and calls for a moratorium on Monsanto's ghastly genetically engineered crops. It advocates buying local and working with fair trade movements against free trade corporate takeovers.[9]

In a number of capitalist countries, governments have taken over ailing private industries and nursed them back to health, testimony to the comparative capacities and objectives of private and public capital:

socialism rescuing capitalism as usual. Immediately after World War II, Western European governments nationalized banks, railways, and natural resources in successful attempts to speed up reconstruction. The French telephone, gas, and electric companies were also public monopolies. Public ownership in France brought such marvels as the high-speed TGV train, superior to trains provided by US capitalism. The not-for-profit publicly owned railroads in France and Italy work far better than the privately owned ones in the United States—which work to the extent they do because of public subsidies.

The state and municipal universities and colleges in the United States are public and therefore "socialist"—shocking news to some of the students who attend them. Some of these schools are among the very best institutions of higher learning in the country; although, because of enormous tuition increases, all of them are becoming less and less affordable and less socialist.

As we saw in Chapter 4, publicly owned utilities in this country are better managed, safer, and less costly than private ones. Since they do not have to produce huge salaries for their CEOs and endless profits for stockholders, their rates are lower and they put millions in earnings back into the general budget, saving taxpayers a lot of expense. In Chapters 5 and 6 we saw how much more affordable and serviceable is socialized medicine compared with the US profit-driven medical system. The British National Health Service, for instance, costs 50 percent less than our for-profit system yet guarantees more reliable medical care. Even though a Tory government during the 1980s imposed budget stringency on British health care "in order to squeeze economies from the system at the expense of quality," a majority of Britons still want to keep their socialized health service.[10]

All the industrialized Western European social democracies provide free medical care, education, and human services for those in need, along with strong government regulations on corporations and financial institutions. Yet citizens of these countries work fewer hours than do Americans and enjoy five- and six-week vacations. They also have far more generous benefits and sick leave policies.[11]

Free marketeers in various countries do what they can to undermine public services by defunding them and eventually privatizing them.[12] The privatization of postal services in New Zealand brought a tidy profit for investors, a rise in postal rates, wage and benefit cuts for postal workers, and a closing of more than a third of the country's post offices: poorer service at higher cost, capitalism rolling back socialism. Likewise, the privatization of telephone and gas utilities in Great Britain resulted in dramatically higher management salaries, soaring rates, and inferior service. Rightist governments rush to privatize because not-for-profit public ownership *does* work—and better than the private utilities.

Most socialists are not against personal-use private property, such as a home. And some are not even against small businesses in the service sector. Nor are most socialists against modest income differentials or special monetary rewards for persons who make outstanding contributions to society.

"It Was Better under Communism"

There is no guarantee that a socialized economy will always succeed. The state-owned economies of Eastern Europe and the former Soviet Union suffered ultimately fatal distortions in their development because of (a) the backlog of poverty and want in the societies they inherited; (b) years of capitalist encirclement, embargo, invasion, devastating wars, and costly Cold War arms buildups; (c) lack of administrative initiative, insufficient technological innovation, and poor incentive systems; and (d) a repressive political rule that allowed little critical feedback. At the same time, it should be acknowledged that the former communist states transformed impoverished semi-feudal countries into relatively advanced societies. Whatever their mistakes and crimes, they achieved what capitalism has no intention of accomplishing: adequate food, housing, and clothing for all; economic security in old age; free medical care; free education at all levels; and a guaranteed adequate income.

As the peoples in these former communist countries are now discovering, the free market means freedom mostly for those who have money and a drastic decline in living standards for most everyone else. With the advent of free market reforms in the former USSR and Eastern Europe, workers saw their real wages, pensions, and savings dissolve. After health and education systems were privatized, the quality of life began to deteriorate. Unemployment, poverty, beggary, homelessness, crime, violence, suicide, mental depression, and prostitution skyrocketed. By 70 and 80 percent majorities, the people in these newly arrived free market countries testify that life had been better under the communists. The breakup of farm collectives and cooperatives and the reversion to private farming caused a 40 percent decline in agricultural productivity in countries like Hungary and East Germany where collective farming actually had performed as well and often better than the heavily subsidized private farming in the West.[13]

The question of what kind of public ownership we should struggle for deserves more treatment than can be given here. American socialism cannot be modeled on the Soviet Union, China, Cuba, or other countries with different historical, economic, and cultural developments. But these countries ought to be examined so that we might learn from their accomplishments, problems, failures, and crimes. Our goal should be an egalitarian, communitarian, environmentally conscious socialism, with a variety of productive forms, offering economic security, political democracy, and vital protection for the ecological system that sustains us.

What is needed to bring about fundamental change is widespread organizing not only around particular issues but for a movement that can project the great necessity for democratic change, a movement ready to embrace new alternatives, including public ownership of major corporations and worker control of production. With time and struggle, we might hope that people will become increasingly intolerant of the growing injustices of the reactionary and inequitable free market system and will move toward a profoundly democratic solution. Perhaps then the day will come, as it came in social orders of the past, when those who seem invincible will be shaken from their pinnacles.

Epilogue
The Next Trip

IMAGINE NOW THAT WE ARE ALL INSIDE one titanic bus hurtling down a road that is headed for a fatal plunge into a deep ravine. What are our profit addicts doing? They are hustling up and down the aisle, selling us crash cushions and seat belts at exorbitant prices. They got an inside tip about the ravine plunge, so they were able to plan ahead for this sales opportunity. Talk about cornering the market: They monopolize the cushions and seat belts and by the time the bus plunges over the rail and into the ravine, they will have sold all their overpriced cushions and seat belts and will have made a killing, if you will excuse the expression.

We have to put aside our consumerism and take action. We have to get up from our seats and place the profiteering hawkers under adult supervision. Then we must rush the front of the bus, yank the driver away, grab hold of the wheel, slow the bus down, and turn it around. Not easy but maybe still possible. With me it is a recurrent scenario.

It should be clear to us that—despite the climate deniers—there is growing restlessness and resistance on the bus. Protests and direct actions against fracking, genetic modification, toxic dumping, nuclear power, wealth inequality, and other potentially catastrophic ecological and economic abuses are growing in numbers.

On the opening page of this book I pointed out how no one predicted the uprisings that boiled over in the Middle East a few years ago and no one predicted the protests within our own country, beginning with Occupy Wall Street in September 2011. The Occupy protest spread across seventy cities and hundreds of other US communities, followed by similar Occupy actions in scores of other countries around the world. The Occupy movement has continued to operate within the United States.

Then, on September 21, 2014, the largest environmental demonstration in history took place in New York. Estimates varied from 400,000 marchers to 600,000, according to police scanners, a massive convergence of hope and anger, a determination to not let Mother Earth—and the rest of us—die a furious death, to not let anyone take us over the cliff for a sack of gold. "People are coming in amazing numbers," exclaimed one demonstration organizer. Union workers and nonunion workers, students and teachers, artists and professionals of every type, community organizers and Grandmas Against Global Warming, almost every occupation and identity compelled by a common concern for survival and betterment.

That same September day in 2014 also saw large protests in Berlin, London, Melbourne, and some 140 other countries, enormous numbers of people determined to turn the bus around, sending a message of resistance to their "leaders."

Democratic action against capitalist despoilment needs to be nurtured—no matter how small and partial and seemingly hopeless it might seem at times. The people must not be satisfied with tinseled favors offered by smooth-talking oligarchs and rapacious free market moguls.

"But they don't care about what we think. They turn a deaf ear to us," some people complain. That is not true. They care very much about what you think. In fact, that is the only thing about you that holds their attention and concern. They don't care if you go hungry, unemployed, sick, or homeless. But they do care when you are beginning to entertain resistant democratic thoughts. They get nervous when you discard your liberal complaints and adopt a radical analysis. They do care that you are catching on as to what the motives and functions of the national security state and the US global empire are all about at home and in so many corners of the world. They get furiously concerned when you and millions like you are rejecting the pap that is served up by corporate media and establishment leaders.

By controlling our perceptions, they control our society; they control public opinion and public discourse. And they limit the range and impact of our political consciousness. The plutocrats know that their power comes from their ability to control our empowering responses. They know they can live at the apex of the social pyramid only as long as they can keep us in line at the pyramid's base. Who pays for all their wars? We do. Who fights these wars? We do or our low-income loved ones do. If we refuse to be led around on a super-patriotic, fear-ridden leash and if we come to our own decisions and act upon them more and more as our ranks grow, then the ruling profiteers' power shrinks and can even unwind and crash—as has happened with dynasties and monarchies of previous epochs.

We need to strive in every way possible for the revolutionary unraveling, a revolution of organized consciousness striking at the empire's heart with full force when democracy is in the streets and mobilized for the kind of irresistible upsurge that seems to come from nowhere yet is sometimes able to carry everything before it.

There is nothing sacred about the existing system. All economic and political institutions are contrivances that should serve the interests of the people. When they fail to do so, they should be replaced by something more responsive, more just, and more democratic.

Notes

Chapter 1

1. Amanda Gilson, Facebook posting, September 2011.
2. Gary Younge, "Working Class Voters: Why America's Poor Are Willing to Vote Republican," *The Guardian,* October 29, 2012.
3. See Paul Krugman's "The Forever Slump," *New York Times,* August 15, 2014.
4. See Chapter 8 for additional remarks regarding wealth distribution.

Chapter 2

1. "A Note on Edmund Morgan," *Yale Alumni Magazine,* September/October 2013, 12.
2. Kirkpatrick Sale, *The Conquest of Paradise* (New York: Knopf, 1990), 304–307.
3. Sale, *The Conquest of Paradise,* 301–304.
4. The literature on the mass liquidation of the Native American nations is substantial. For instance, see Sale, *The Conquest of Paradise*; David E. Stannard, *American Holocaust: The Conquest of the New World* (Oxford: Oxford University Press, 1993); Dale Van Every, *Disinherited* (New York: Avon Books, 1966); and

Francis Jennings, *The Invasion of America: Indians, Colonialism, and the Cant of Conquest* (New York: Norton, 1976). On the closing years of the Indian wars, see Dee Brown, *Bury My Heart at Wounded Knee* (New York: Bantam Books, 1972), especially 413–418 for the 1890 massacre. There were a few other minor encounters and skirmishes immediately afterward, for instance, the Drexel Mission Fight, but Wounded Knee is generally treated as the final real battle.

5. Indigenous peoples of Alaska were popularly known as "Eskimos," a term that is still in use. They are more properly referred to collectively as "Alaskan Natives." For some strange reason, many progressives in the United States refer to all Alaskan Natives as "Inuits," even though the Inuit are only one of the Native Alaskan peoples, along with the Aleut, Alutiiq, Athabascan, Iñupiat, Cup'ik, Haida, Tlingit, and Yup'ik. Calling all of these Native Alaskans "Inuits" would be like referring to all Native American Indians as Cherokee.

6. S. Brian Willson, "American Exceptionalism: The Rhetoric and the Reality," *War Crimes Times*, Winter 2014.

7. John Kozy, "Violence: The American Way of Life," *Global Research*, November 15, 2013.

8. Phillips' *American Negro Slavery*, originally published in 1918, remains in print today; see also Eugene D. Genovese and Elizabeth Fox-Genovese, *Fatal Self-Deception: Slaveholding Paternalism in the Old South* (Cambridge: Cambridge University Press, 2011).

9. See the testimonials of slaves in James Mellon (ed.), *Bullwhip Days: The Slaves Remember* (London: Weidenfeld and Nicolson, 1988). For revealing portraits of slaves from different eras, see Jacqueline Jones, *A Dreadful Deceit* (New York: Basic Books, 2013).

10. Jack Gratus, *The Great White Lie: Slavery, Emancipation, and Changing Racial Attitudes* (New York: Monthly Review Press, 1973), 38, 52–53, 71; and Charles H. Nichols, *Many Thousand Gone* (Bloomington: Indiana University Press, 1963), 3–13.

11. Herbert Aptheker, *American Negro Slave Revolts* (New York: International Publishers, 1987), passim.

12. James Thomas Flexner, "Washington and Slavery," *Constitution*, 3 (Spring-Summer 1991).

13. Frederick Douglass, *My Bondage and My Freedom* (New York: Dover Publications, 1969), 85.

14. Henry Louis Gates Jr., "Not Gone With the Wind: Voices of Slavery,"

New York Times, February 9, 2003. On the special tribulations of female slaves, see Deborah Gray White, *Ain't I a Woman? Female Slaves in the Plantation South* (New York: Norton, 1985); and Melton A. McLaurin, *Celia, A Slave* (Athens: University of Georgia Press, 1991).

15. James L. Roark, *Masters without Slaves: Southern Planters in the Civil War and Reconstruction* (New York: Norton, 1977), 97ff; also Mellon, *Bullwhip Days,* passim.

16. This dispute about the profitability of slavery is treated in Robert William Fogel and Stanley L. Engerman, *Time on the Cross: The Economics of American Slavery,* reissued edition (New York: Norton, 2013).

17. Edward E. Baptist, *The Half Has Never Been Told: Slavery and the Making of American Capitalism* (New York: Basic Books, 2014).

18. See Craig Steven Wilder, *Ebony and Ivy: Race, Slavery, and the Troubled History of America's Universities* (New York: Bloomsbury Press, 2013); and Baptist, *The Half Has Never Been Told.*

19. Allegra di Bonaventura, "The Chains of Academe," *Wall Street Journal,* January 2, 2014; also Wilder, *Ebony and Ivy.*

20. This treatment of post-Reconstruction slavery is drawn from Douglas A. Blackmon, *Slavery by Another Name: The Re-Enslavement of Black Americans from the Civil War to World War II* (New York: Anchor Books, 2008).

21. Blackmon, *Slavery by Another Name,* 6–9, 96–97, and passim.

22. For further discussion of racist myths and practices, see Michael Parenti, *The Culture Struggle* (New York: Seven Stories Press, 2006), 91 *ff.* On the prevalence of racism in America, see Tim Wise, *Between Barack and a Hard Place: Racism and White Denial in the Age of Obama* (San Francisco: City Lights, 2009).

23. Michelle Alexander, *The New Jim Crow: Mass Incarceration in the Age of Colorblindness,* reprint edition (New York: New Press, 2012).

24. See Pamela Brown, "Can We Have Capitalism without Racism? The Invisible Chains of Debt and the Catastrophic Loss of African American Wealth," AlterNet.org, January 4, 2014.

25. See Peter Munch's work on Norwegian immigrant acculturation and related subjects; for instance, his "Segregation and Assimilation of Norwegian Settlement in Wisconsin," *Norwegian-American Studies* 18 (1955): 102. Available at NAHA Online, www.naha.stolaf.edu.

26. Susie J. Pak, *Gentlemen Bankers: The World of J. P. Morgan* (Cambridge, MA: Harvard University Press, 2013).

27. Terry Golway, *Machine Made: Tammany Hall and the Creation of Modern American Politics* (New York: Liveright, 2014); and Edward Kosner, "From Bosses to Czars," *Wall Street Journal*, March 10, 2014.

28. James R. Barrett, *The Irish Way: Becoming American in the Multiethnic City* (New York: Penguin, 2013); see also Jay P. Dolan, *The Irish Americans: A History* (New York: Bloomsbury, 2010).

29. Goddard cited in Suketu Mehta, "The Superiority Complex," *Time*, February 3, 2014.

30. See Felipe Fernandez-Armesto, *Our America: A Hispanic History of the United States* (New York: Norton, 2014).

31. See Michael Parenti, *The Faces of Imperialism* (Boulder, CO: Paradigm, 2011).

Chapter 3

1. The literature on this history is immense. Consider as a sampling: Michael Parenti, *The Face of Imperialism* (Boulder, CO: Paradigm, 2011); Eduardo Galeano, *Open Veins of Latin America: Five Centuries of the Pillage of a Continent* (New York: Monthly Review Press, 1973); L. S. Stavrianos, *Global Rift: The Third World Comes of Age* (New York: William Murrow, 1981); Mike Davis, *Late Victorian Holocausts* (New York: Verso, 2001); Carl Boggs, *The Crimes of Empire* (London: Pluto Press, 2010).

2. William Blum, *The Anti-Empire Report*, September 1, 2010, www.killinghope.org.

3. On that last example, see Stephen Lendman (ed.), *Flashpoint in Ukraine: How the U.S. Drive for Hegemony Risks World War III* (Atlanta: Clarity Press, 2014).

4. For expanded overviews of how global capitalism works, see Parenti, *The Face of Imperialism*, and James Petras and Henry Veltmeyer (with Luciano Vasapollo and Mauro Casadio), *Empire with Imperialism: The Globalizing Dynamics of Neoliberal Capitalism* (Black Point, Nova Scotia: Fernwood Publishing/Zed Books, 2005).

5. Abraham Falls, *Human Trafficking: A Global Perspective of Modern Day Human Trafficking and Sex Slavery* (Amazon Digital Services, 2014).

6. On the global expansion of labor exploitation in this era of high-tech

imperialism, see Fred Goldstein, *Low-Wage Capitalism* (New York: World View Forum, 2008); see also Bud Meyers, "Record Earnings but Offshoring (Is Still) Hurting Workers," *Daily Kos,* www.dailykos.com, June 28, 2013.

7. Walter Rodney, *How Europe Underdeveloped Africa* (Baltimore: Black Classic Press, 2011).

8. Ernest Mandel, *Marxist Economic Theory,* vol. 2 (New York: Monthly Review Press, 1970), especially Chapter 13.

9. Mike Davis, *Late Victorian Holocausts: El Nino Famines and the Making of the Third World* (New York: Verso, 2002).

10. Timothy Parsons, *The Rule of Empire* (Oxford: Oxford University Press, 2010).

11. For a recent example, see Stephen Lendman (ed.), *Flashpoint in Ukraine: How the US Drive for Hegemony Risks World War III* (Atlanta: Clarity Press, 2014).

12. For a more comprehensive listing of US overthrow of other governments, see William Blum, Peter Scott, and Larry Bleidner, *Killing Hope: U.S. Military and CIA Interventions Since World War II* (Monroe, ME: Common Courage Press, 1995).

13. Elizabeth Malkin, "Trial on Guatemalan Civil War Carnage Leaves Out U.S. Role," *New York Times,* May 16, 2013.

14. Michael Parenti, *God and His Demons* (Prometheus, 2010), 202, 209.

15. Antonio M. Taguba, "Stop the CIA Spin on the Senate Torture Report," *New York Times,* August 6, 2014.

Chapter 4

1. For accounts and testimonies regarding the San Bruno disaster, see *San Francisco Chronicle,* September 10–12, 2010.

2. The Utility Reform Network (TURN) report, November 2010.

3. George Avalos, "PG&E Should Be Fined $13 Million for Record Keeping Blunders," *Oakland Tribune,* September 27, 2013.

4. Steve Johnson, et al, "Federal Agency Blames PG&E," *Oakland Tribune,* August 31, 2011.

5. PG&E Accidents Timeline, 21st Century, 2001–2014.

6. Demian Bulwa, "40 Years of Unsafe Pressure," *San Francisco Chronicle,* May 26, 2012.

7. *Contra Costa Times*, editorial, December 19, 2011.

8. Jaxon Van Derbeken, "Mayor: Utilities Overseer Must Go," *San Francisco Chronicle*, July 29, 2014.

9. Cassandra Sweet, "U.S. Readies Criminal Charges for Pipeline Blast," *Wall Street Journal*, March 28, 2014.

10. "PG&E Customers to Foot Part of Pipe Safety Costs," *Epoch Times*, December 27, 2012–January 2, 2013.

11. Eric Nalder and Jaxon Van Derbeken, "Law Puts Pipeline Records Off-Limits," *San Francisco Chronicle*, November 27, 2011.

12. Michael Kanellos, "Peter Darbee, PG&E's Green CEO, Steps Down Amid Mistakes," *CSweek*, 5–9, 2014.

13. *Contra Costa Times*, September 27, 2010.

14. Marc Lifsher, "Edison Again Says Customers Should Help Pay for San Onofre," *Los Angeles Times*, October 14, 2013.

15. TURN report, n.d., circa January 2012.

16. *San Francisco Chronicle*, August 16, 2012.

17. Quoted in Pat Barile, "Where Production Benefits Workers," *Daily World*, September 20, 1984.

18. See Kanellos, "Peter Darbee, PG&E's Green CEO, Steps Down."

19. Robert Gammon, "PG&E to Increase Fracking," *East Bay Express*, August 17–23, 2011.

20. TURN, "Fact Sheet," n.d.

Chapter 5

1. Joseph Mercola, "Death from Prescription Drugs: The New Epidemic Sweeping across America," Mercola.com, October 26, 2011.

2. *New York Times*, December 16, 2011.

3. *New York Times*, December 16, 2011.

4. See the report by Elizabeth Rosenthal, *New York Times*, December 2, 2013.

5. *San Francisco Business Times*, January 7, 2014.

6. Julie Creswell et al., "Hospital Charges Surge for Common Ailments, Data Shows," *New York Times*, June 3, 2014.

7. *Healthcare-NOW!* (newsletter), December 1, 2011.

8. Steven Brill, "Bungling the Easy Stuff," *Time*, December 16, 2013.

9. *New York Times*, May 8, 2013; *Wall Street Journal*, May 9, 2013.
10. *New York Times*, June 23, 2012.
11. Elizabeth Rosenthal, "Doctor's Salaries Are Not the Big Cost," *New York Times*, May 18, 2014.
12. The Institute of Medicine report is cited in Marty Makary, "The Cost of Chasing Cancer," *Time*, March 10, 2014.
13. On excessive radiation, see W. Gifford-Jones, "I'm Sorry, I Don't Know How Much Radiation Is Given," *Epoch Times*, February 8–14, 2007. On pharmaceuticals, see Ben Goldacre, *Bad Pharma: How Drug Companies Mislead Doctors and Harm Patients* (London: Faber and Faber, 2013).
14. William Charney, "The Carnage Continues, Part 2," *Z Magazine*, September 2012 [italics added].
15. "Industry Lobbies to Weaken Medical Devise Oversight," *Public Citizen* (Health Letter), April 2012.
16. Dr. Daniel Benjamin of Duke University, quoted in "Many Drugs Given to Children Tested Only for Adults," *Epoch Times*, March 22, 2007.
17. Trust for America's Health (Washington), "Harper's Index," *Harper's*, December 2012.
18. Marty Makary, *Unaccountable: What Hospitals Won't Tell You and How Transparency Can Revolutionize Health Care* (New York: Bloomsbury, 2013).
19. See, for instance, maternity care: Elisabeth Rosenthal, "American Way of Birth, Costliest in the World," *New York Times*, July 1, 2013.
20. Jim Hightower, "Outrage of the Month!" *Public Citizen* (Health Letter), April 2012.
21. *Commonwealth Health Care Report*, June 2014.

Chapter 6

1. Names of all correspondents have been changed for privacy purposes.
2. The "donut hole" is a coverage gap in prescription drugs lasting for a year-long period or so. After Medicare beneficiaries exit the initial coverage period of the prescription drug plan, they become financially responsible entirely on their own for a higher prescription cost until they reach the "catastrophic-coverage threshold." In other words, the donut hole can hurt you hard (financially) but since it lasts only a year, it supposedly does not totally destroy you.

3. *Time,* June 20, 2011.

4. AIG is American International Group, an insurance cartel that invests heavily in medical liability research to develop "more effective and affordable coverage," so they claim.

Chapter 7

1. Colin Jenkins, "Coming Home to Roost, Part 1: Militarism, War Culture, and Police Brutality," *Z Magazine,* April 2014.

2. *New York Times,* March 28, 2010.

3. "Polish Pedophile Priest Jailed for 8.5 Years," GMANEWS online, December 3, 2013.

4. See Thomas P. Doyle, A.W. Richard Sipe, and Patrick Wall, *Sex, Priests, and Secret Codes: The Catholic Church's 2,000-Year Paper Trail of Sexual Abuse* (Los Angeles: Bonus Books, 2006); DCA Hillman, *Original Sin: Ritual Child Rape and the Church* (Berkeley, CA: Ronin Publishing, 2012); Karen Liebreich, *Fallen Order: Intrigue, Heresy, and Scandal in the Rome of Galileo and Caravaggio* (New York: Grove Press, 2004).

5. Stacy Meichtry, "Vatican Opens Investigation Into Legion of Christ Priests," *Wall Street Journal,* May 12–13, 2012.

6. Associated Press report, April 28, 2014; Jason Berry and Gerald Renner, *Vows of Silence: The Abuse of Power in the Papacy of John Paul II* (New York: Free Press, 2004); and Berry's report in *San Francisco Chronicle,* April 10, 2005.

7. Press coverage in recent years has been substantial. Here is a relatively lean sampling of stories covering the points listed above: Michael D'Antonio, *Mortal Sins: Sex, Crime and the Era of Catholic Scandal* (New York: Thomas Dunne Books/ St. Martin's Press, 2014); Laurie Goodstein, "Audit Finds Sex Abuse Was Topic Decades Ago," *New York Times,* June 19, 2013; Sharon Otterman, "In Interview, Priest Suggests Abuse Victims Are to Blame," *New York Times,* August 31, 2012; David Edward, "Catholic Newspaper Scrubs Interview After Priest Says Children Are 'Seducers,'" *The Raw Story,* August 30, 2012; Bill Berkowitz, "The Catholic Church's Worldwide Sexual Abuse Scandal," *Z Magazine,* April 2013; Laurie Goodstein, "Cardinal Authorized Payments to Abusers," *New York Times,* May 31, 2012; Laurie Goodstein, "Church Whistle-Blowers Join Forces on Abuse," *New York Times,* May 21, 2013; Peter Loftus, "Top Priest: 'Did Best I Could,'"

Wall Street Journal, May 24, 2012 ; David Gibson, "U.S. Bishops Still Stonewall on Sex Abuse," *Wall Street Journal,* June 8, 2012.

8. Jane Kramer, "Holy Orders," *New Yorker,* May 2, 2005; Gary MacEoin, *The People's Church* (New York: Crossroad, 1996).

9. Investigative Staff of the *Boston Globe, Betrayal: The Crisis in the Catholic Church* (Boston: Little, Brown, 2002), 162.

10. Jason Berry, *Render unto Rome: The Secret Life of Money in the Catholic Church* (New York: Crown, 2011), 215 and passim.

11. Doyle, Sipe, and Wall, *Sex, Priests, and Secret Codes;* Sharon Smith, "The Hypocrites in the Catholic Church," *Socialist Worker,* March 5, 2004.

12. *New York Times,* May 24, 2014.

13. Karen Liebreich, *Fallen Order* (New York: Grove Press, 2004), 263, 266.

14. *New York Times,* April 22, 2010.

15. Jason Berry, "Vatican Cardinal Bucked U.S. Bishop on Abuse," *National Catholic Reporter,* April 22, 2010.

16. Elizabetta Povoledo, "Pope Francis to Meet Victims of Sexual Abuse," *New York Times,* May 27, 2014.

17. *New York Times,* April 12, 2010.

18. Christa Brown, "When Will SBC Address Clergy Sex Abuse," ABPNEWS/HERALD, www.BaptistNews.com, April 12, 2013.

19. *Sacramento Bee,* July 15, 2006.

20. For a more detailed discussion, see Michael Parenti, *God and His Demons* (Amherst, NY: Prometheus, 2010) 150–153.

21. iamthewitness.com. (n.d.)

22. http://www.jlaw.com/Articles/mesiralaw2.html.

23. Ray Rivera, "Brooklyn Prosecutor Defends Record on Abuse Cases," *New York Times,* May 17, 2012; Sharon Otterman, "4 Ultra-Orthodox Jews Charged with Trying to Silence Accuser in Sex Abuse Case," *New York Times,* June 22, 2012.

24. Sharon Otterman, "Chemical Thrown at Rabbi Who Aided Victims of Abuse," *New York Times,* December 12, 2012. A once-prominent cantor in the Brooklyn ultra-Orthodox community, Baruch Lebovits pleaded guilty to sexual molestation and was sentenced to ten to thirty-two years, a case that was thrown out on a technicality: *New York Times,* June 18, 2013, and May 17, 2014.

25. Vivian Yee, "Report of 80s Sexual Abuse Rattles Yeshiva Campus," *New York Times,* December 14, 2012.

26. Melvyn Goldstein, William Siebenschuh, and Tashi-Tsering, *The Struggle for Modern Tibet*: *The Autobiography of Tashi-Tsering* (New York: M. E. Sharpe, 1997), passim.

27. Michael Parenti, *The Culture Struggle* (New York: Seven Stories Press, 2006), 67.

28. Nick Cumming-Bruce, "Vatican Tells of 848 Priests Ousted in Decade," *New York Times*, May 7, 2014.

29. Associated Press, June 11, 2004.

30. Lijia Zhang, "Child Abuse in China," *New York Times*, May 2, 2014; also "Chinese Schoolchildren at Risk of Sexual Abuse," *New China Magazine*, August 2013.

31. See Saeed Kamali Dehghan's report in *The Guardian*, June 19, 2014.

32. Elizabeth Fernandez and Stephanie Salter, "Ugly Americans: Sex Tourists," *San Francisco Chronicle*, February 17, 2003; Andrew Cockburn, "21st Century Slavery," *National Geographic*, September 2003.

33. Lisa Manshel, *Nap Time: The True Story of Sexual Abuse at a Suburban Daycare Center* (New York: Zebra Books, 1990); Ross E. Cheit, *The Witch-Hunt Narrative: Politics, Psychology and the Sexual Abuse of Children* (Oxford: Oxford University Press, 2014); Daniel Ryder, *Breaking the Circle of Satanic Ritual Abuse* (Minneapolis: CompCare, 1992); Margaret Smith, *Ritual Abuse* (San Francisco: HarperSanFrancisco, 1993).

34. Marc Fisher, "The Master," *New Yorker*, April 1, 2013; Maureen Dowd, "Moral Dystopia," *New York Times*, June 17, 2012.

35. Campbell Brown, "Keeping Sex Predators Out of Schoolrooms," *Wall Street Journal*, January 17, 2014.

36. Associate Press, October 3, 2007; http://www.boyscoutabuse.com.

37. Kirk Johnson, "Newly Released Boy Scout Files Give Glimpse into 20 Years of Sexual Abuse," *New York Times*, October 19, 2012; www.rawstory.com/rs/2012/12/13.

38. Frank Bruni, "The Molester Next Door," *New York Times*, November 8, 2011; Maureen Dowd, "Personal Foul at Penn State," *New York Times*, November 9, 2011.

39. Frank Bruni, "Suffer the Children," *New York Times*, September 11, 2012.

40. Sarah Lyall, "BBC Faces New Claims of Sex Abuse," *New York Times*, May 31, 2013.

41. Nina Burleigh, "Creative License: 'Great Men' Get a Pass from their

Peers," *New York Observer,* February 10, 2014; Mia Farrow, *What Falls Away* (New York: Nan Talese, 1997); Nicole Drawc, "Michael Jackson Really Was a Pedophile?" *Guardian Liberty Voice,* May 13, 2014.

42. Richard Riis' report, *Daily Kos,* June 8, 2014.

43. Lori Heise, "When Women Are Prey," *Washington Post,* December 8, 1991.

44. David Paquette, letter to *New York Times,* November 10, 2011.

45. Anne-Marie Hislop, letter to *New York Times,* June 15, 2012.

46. Louise Armstrong, *Kiss Daddy Tonight* (New York: Pocket Books, 1985); Louise Armstrong, *Rocking the Cradle of Sexual Politics: What Happened When Women Said Incest* (Boston: Addison-Wesley, 1994); Eve Ensler and Stacey Schrader, "Childhood Sexual Abuse" Special Issue, *Central Park* 22 (Spring 1993); Charlotte Vale Allen, *Daddy's Girl* (New York: Berkley Books, 1982); Larry Wolff, *Child Abuse in Freud's Vienna* (New York: New York University Press, 1995); Nancy L. Carlson and Kathryn Quina, *Rape, Incest, and Sexual Harassment: A Guide for Helping Survivors* (Santa Barbara, CA: Praeger, 1989).

Chapter 8

1. Oxford International Report, "The 85 Richest People in the World Have As Much Wealth As the 3.5 Billion Poorest," *Working for the Few,* January 23, 2014.

2. Matthew G. Miller and Peter Newcomb, "Billionaires Worth $1.9 Trillion Seek Advantage in 2013," *Bloomberg,* January 2, 2013; and "Globally Almost 870 Million Chronically Undernourished," report by United Nations Food and Agricultural Organization, October 9, 2012.

3. Josh Boak, "One in Three Americans in Debt Collection," *Epoch Times,* July 31–August 6, 2014 (reprint from the Associated Press, n.d.).

4. Susan George, *A Fate Worse Than Debt: The World Financial Crisis and the Poor* (New York: Grove Press, 1990).

5. Peter Dreier, "What Housing Recovery?" *New York Times,* May 9, 2014.

6. Chelsey Dulaney, "Rents Rise 0.8% as Incomes Stagnate," *Wall Street Journal,* July 2, 2014.

7. See, for instance, Andre Vltchek, *Indonesia: Archipelago of Fear* (London: Pluto, 2012).

8. Gerald Colby, *Dupont: Behind the Nylon Curtain* (Fort Lee, NJ: Lyle Stuart, 2005).

9. Oxford International Report, "The 85 Richest People in the World."

10. *USA Today*, January 20, 2014.

11. National Alliance to End Homelessness, *The State of Homelessness in America 2014*, Report, May 27, 2014.

12. Roger Thurow and Scott Kilman, *Enough: Why the World's Poorest Starve in an Age of Plenty*, reprint edition (New York: Public Affairs, 2010).

13. Annie Lowery, "Income Gap, Meet the Longevity Gap," *New York Times*, March 15, 2014; also Peter Edelman, *So Rich, So Poor: Why It's So Hard to End Poverty in America* (New York: New Press, 2013).

14. Illiteracy: World Illiteracy Rates, Infoplease.com. (drawn from a UNICEF report).

15. Robert Longley, "The US Federal Minimum Wage," About.com, US Government, June 23, 2014.

16. Joseph Shapiro, "In Ferguson, Court Fines and Fees Fuel Anger," www.NPR.org, August 25, 2014.

17. Derek Thompson, "How the Rich Shall Inherit the Earth," *The Atlantic*, June 2014.

18. Edward N. Wolff, "The Asset Price Meltdown and the Wealth of the Middle Class," National Bureau of Economic Research, Working Paper 18559 (November 2012).

19. "Wealth Inequality in America," *Solidarity*, May/June 2013, 14.

20. Neil Shah, "U.S. Wealth Rises, But Not All Benefit," *Wall Street Journal*, March 7, 2014; Paul Wiseman, "Richest 1 percent earn biggest share since '20s," www.miamiheraldlcom, September 10, 2013.

21. See Thompson, "How the Rich Shall Inherit the Earth."

22. Carl Herman, "1% hide $21 trillion, US big banks hide $10 trillion; ending world poverty: $3 trillion," July 24, 2012.

23. "The Sorry State of Corporate Taxes," *Just Taxes* (ITEP and CTJ Newsletter), Spring 2014.

24. Marketwatch.com, December 5, 2013.

25. Peter Mathews, *Dollar Democracy: with Liberty and Justice for Some*, www.epetermathews.com, Chapter 8.

26. Annie Lowrey, "The Wealth Gap in America Is Growing, Too," *New York Times*, April 2, 2014. Lowrey draws from work by Thomas Piketty, Gabriel Zucman,

and Emmanuel Saez. For a thorough study of wealth inequality, see Thomas Piketty, *Capital in the Twenty-First Century* (Cambridge, MA: Belknap, 2014).

27. Jordan Melograna, "Workers Resist Scofflaw Employers in Wage Theft Capital of the US," *Truthout*, July 2, 2014; Sam Levin, "Berkeley Sides with Living Wage Violators," *East Bay Express*, July 9–15, 2014.

28. Jennifer Medina, "Hardship Makes a New Home in the Suburbs," *New York Times*, May 10, 2014.

29. Medina, "Hardship Makes a New Home in the Suburbs"; also Annie Lowrey, "Changed Life of the Poor: Squeak By, and Buy a Lot," *New York Times*, May 1, 2014.

30. Auriandra, "Someone finally polled the 1%—And it's not pretty," *Daily Kos*, May 29, 2014.

31. "Zero sum" means there is no community of interest between two groups. The gains for one come as a loss to the other and vice versa.

Chapter 9

1. Gregg Jones, *Honor in the Dust: Theodore Roosevelt, War in the Philippines, and the Rise and Fall of America's Imperial Dream* (New York: New American Library, 2012).

2. Howard K. Beale, *Theodore Roosevelt and the Rise of America to World Power* (New York: Collier Books, 1962).

3. Robert H. Wiebe, *The Search for Order 1877–1920* (New York: Hill and Wang, 1967); Rhonda F. Levine, *Class Struggle and the New Deal: Industrial Labor, Industrial Capital, and the State* (Lawrence: University Press of Kansas, 1988).

4. Two decades later Argentina was still gripped in defaults and write-downs; see Mary Anastasia O'Grady, "The Argentine Bond Mess Gets Messier," *Wall Street Journal*, July 14, 2014.

5. George L. Kenney, "Enron, Kenneth Lay, Jeffrey Skilling, Andrew Fastow—How Do They Compare to Today's Economic Crisis," www.EzineArticles.com, October 8, 2008.

6. Erin Arvedlund, *Too Good to Be True: The Rise and Fall of Bernie Madoff* (New York: Portfolio, 2009); Jerry Oppenheimer, *Madoff with the Money* (New York: Wiley, 2009).

7. "Alan Greenspan: What I Got Wrong," interview with Anthony Mason, www.CBSNews.com, October 20, 2013.

8. Karl Marx, *Capital*, vol. 1, Chapter 32.

9. Bob Ivry, Bradley Keoun, and Phil Kuntz, "Secret Fed Loans Gave Banks $13 Billion Undisclosed to Congress," *Bloomberg*, November 27, 2011.

10. *Wall Street Journal*, June 23, 2014, July 1, 2014, and July 26–27, 2014.

11. Michael Parenti, *Democracy for the Few* (Independence, KY: Wadsworth, 2011), 23–26.

12. Penny Colman, *Rosie the Riveter: Women Working on the Home Front in World War II* (Chicago: Raintree Fusion, 2008).

13. "GI" stood for "Government Issue," the shorthand military label given to enlisted men in the US Army during World War II. Various articles issued in conformity with US military regulations were stamped "GI," as with GI soap and GI clothes. Eventually reference was made to GI soldiers, meaning enlisted men. Finally the soldier himself was designated a GI.

14. See James F. Tracy, "Plutocracy, Poverty, and Prosperity," *Censored 2014* (New York: Seven Stories Press, 2013), 96 and passim.

15. See the discussion on empire in Chapter 3.

16. See Michael Harrington, *The Other America: Poverty in the United States*, reprint edition (New York: Scribner, 1997).

17. Tracy, "Plutocracy, Poverty, and Prosperity," *Censored 2014*, 88–89; Lewis F. Powell Jr. to Eugene B. Sydnor Jr, "Confidential Memorandum: Attack on American Free Enterprise System," August 23, 1971, cited in Tracy, "Plutocracy, Poverty, and Prosperity," 98.

Chapter 10

1. "BP Oil Spill Timeline," www.theguardian.com, July 22, 2010; Mat McDermott, "Madness: BP Left Off Second Emergency Cutoff and When Do We Say 'Enough'?" www.treehugger.com, May 4, 2010.

2. See, for instance, Jim Galloway, "'Green Police' and the American Mood," www.ajc.com/political insider, February 8, 2010.

3. New parents in the United States are guaranteed their jobs for twelve weeks after the birth of a new baby, thanks to the Family Medical Leave Act of 1993, but their employers are under no obligation to pay parental leave: "Paid

Parental Leave: U.S. vs. the World," www.huffingtonpost.com, February 4, 2013. Lesotho, Swaziland, and Papua New Guinea are the only other countries besides the United States that do not give paid parental leave. Many countries give new fathers paid time off as well or allow parents to share paid leave.

4. About that last one, see Emily Main, "Genetically Modified Foods Labeling, Untested, Unlabeled, and You're Eating It," www.rodalenews.com, October 3, 2011.

5. Cartoonist Robert Mankoff, Conde Nast Publications/www.cartoonbank.com.

6. http://www.mcclatchydc.com/2011/05/24/114695/as-ice-melts-and-technology-improves.html#ixzz1OI7Nfhai.

7. Rozanne Enerson Junker, *The Bank of North Dakota: An Experiment in State Ownership* (McKinleyville, CA: Fithian Press, 1989).

8. For democratic economic alternatives, see Gar Alperovitz, *America beyond Capitalism: Reclaiming Our Wealth, Our Liberty, and Our Democracy* (New York: Wiley, 2006).

9. Organic Consumer Association, www.organicconsumers.org.

10. *New York Times*, June 3, 1987.

11. Jeremy Rifkin, *The European Dream: How Europe's Vision of the Future Is Quietly Eclipsing the American Dream* (New York: Tarcher, 2005); Robert G. Kaiser, "Why Can't We Be More Like Finland?" *Seattle Times*, September 25, 2005 (originally published in the *Washington Post*).

12. See, for instance, Tor Wennerberg, "Undermining the Welfare State in Sweden," *Z Magazine*, June 1995.

13. See Michael Parenti, *Blackshirts and Reds: Rational Fascism and the Overthrow of Communism* (San Francisco: City Lights Books, 1997), Chapters 6 and 7; Michael Parenti, *To Kill a Nation: The Attack on Yugoslavia* (New York: Verso, 2000), Chapters 18 and 19.

Index

Accountability: capitalist system, 120–123
Acculturation of Native Americans, 15
Aetna Insurance, 63
Affordable Care Act, 61–62
Afghanistan, war in, 33–34
Afinator, 73–74
Africa: enslavement, 16–17; massacre by western colonizers, 26
African Americans: victimization during Reconstruction, 19–20; victimization of the working poor, 107
AIDS, 62
Alaska natives, 152(n5)
Allen, Woody, 98
Alta Bates Summit Medical Center, 57–61, 68, 70
American Boychoir School, Princeton, 96–97
American International Group (AIG), 158(n4)
American Revolution, 119
Anglo-Protestant culture: America as, 11; early ethnic settlements, 21; ethnic and class hierarchies, 24; financial elites, 21–22

Anticommunism, 38
Arab Spring, 4, 148
Arawak people, 13
Aristotle, 23
Armenian massacre, 26
Asian immigrants, 23
Assimilation of Native Americans, 15

Banks: "too big to fail," 124; Anglo-Protestant culture, 21–22; mortgage lending, 103; nationalization, 126; public banks, 141–142; tax shelters for the super rich, 109
Beggary, 111
Benedict XVI, 92–93
Boy Scouts of America, 97
Britain: ethnic settlements, 21–22
British Broadcasting System (BBC), 98
British National Health Service, 66, 143
Buddhism, 40
Buffet, Warren, 109–110
Bush, George W., 121–122

California Public Utilities Commission (PUC), 46–56

168 Index

Campaign finance: electoral control by the corporate sector, 54, 110
Canada: health services, 73–74, 76–77
Cancer: European medical care, 75; insurance coverage for treatment, 69–70, 72–73; lack of medical insurance for treatment, 62, 74; PG&E smart meters, 54–55
Capital accumulation, 28–29
Capitalism: addictive nature of, 134; class power and, 9–10; creating poverty, 128–131; environmental degradation by corporate interests, 134; function and responsibility of the capitalist state, 117–118; lack of accountability and transparency, 120–123; Occupy Wall Street movement, 4–5, 108, 148; self-destruction and chronic instability, 123–125; socialism and, 141–146; using the state to protect the capitalist system, 118–120
Castrillón, Dario, 91
Catholic Church: Irish immigrants, 22; pedophilia, 85–93
Chevron Corporation, 52–53
Child brides, 96
Children, sexual molestation of, 84–95
China: maternity leave, 136; pedophilia, 96
Church of Latter-Day Saints (Mormons), 97
Civil War, 16, 18–19
Class: African enslavement, 16–20; American class war, 110; as demographic trait, 8; class power and wealth, 8–10; class warfare, 5–7; ethnic differences and class interests, 23; great class divide, 4–5; health system mirroring class systems, 61–63; Occupy movement, 4; wealth inequality, 101–104

Climate crisis, 138–139, 148
Clinton, Hillary, 140
Cold War, 127–128, 130, 144–146
Colonialism, 11, 26, 31–33
Columbus, Christopher, 15
Communism, 38–39, 53, 85–86, 128, 144–146
Competition, free-enterprise, 122–123
Confederate apologists, 16
Congo, Democratic Republic of the, 26
Cooperatives, producer- and consumer-owned, 142
Corporate sector: class warfare, 6–7; electoral control, 54, 110; environmental degradation, 133–134; foreign policy goals, 40–41; healthcare profits, 62–63; lack of income tax for, 109–110; PG&E, 46–56; plundering the capitalist system, 120–121; profiteering overwhelming environmental responsibility, 139–140; profits as objective, 54–56; propaganda glorifying private enterprise, 45–46; richest billionaires in the world, 104. *See also* Imperialism
Coups d'état, 35
Culture: acculturation of Native Americans, 15

Darbee, Peter, 51–52
Death: hospital-borne infections, 70; medical errors, 64–65, 70–72
Debt, 102–103, 142
Democracy: action against capitalist despoilment, 148–149; free-market plundering, 121; social democracies, 129
Demographic trait, class as, 8–10
Demographics: Native American population decline, 13

Index   169

Denmark: minimum wage, 107
Dental care, 78
Diplomatic immunity for pedophile priests, 89–90
Disability benefits, 75
Disease: antibiotics associated with surgery, 58–59; exposure of Native Americans by white Europeans, 12–13; smart meters, 54–55; the Poorer Half, 106; uninsured citizens, 62
Domestic servitude, 95–96
Donut hole, 157(n2)
Douglass, Frederick, 17

Economic crises: Great Depression, 119–120, 126; Great Recession (2007–2008), 8, 111, 121–124; recession (1900–1915), 119; recessions, 122–123
Economic status: capital accumulation through resource acquisition, 28–29; profitability of slavery, 17–18
Education: African slaves, 16; as soft imperialism, 40; Christianization of Native American children, 12; GI Bill, 127; pedophilia in China, 96; pedophilia in the US, 96–97; sexual molestation by Orthodox rabbis, 94–95; sexual molestation on university campuses, 97; slavery advantaging elite colleges, 18; socialist and capitalist systems, 143; the Poorer Half's lack of, 106
Egypt: Arab Spring uprising, 4
Elites, financial: Anglo-Protestant culture, 21
Energy companies. *See* Pacific Gas and Electric (PG&E)
Enron Corporation, 121
Environmental degradation: capital accumulation and, 134–136; climate crisis, 138–139; demonstrations, 148; profiteering and, 139–140; public services and private services, 136–138
Errors, medical, 64–65, 70–72
Eskimos, 152(n5)
Ethnicity: attack on indigenous cultures, 12–15; obliteration of immigrant cultures, 20–24
Eugenics, 23
Europe: clerical abuse, 85–86; early ethnic settlements, 21–23; health care, 75–78; maternity leave, 136; minimum wage, 107; social democracies, 129
Exploitation: African enslavement, 16–20; objectification and victimization, 84–85; of the poor, 111; racism and sexism, 9; underdevelopment and, 31–32

Families: parental leave, 136, 165(n3); sexual predators among, 84–85, 93–94, 98–100; treatment of female slaves, 17
Family Medical Leave Act (1993), 165(n3)
Federal Reserve, 122
Food stamps, 107, 111–112
Force, superiority of, 38–39
Fox News, 67–68
Fracking, 55
France: African massacres, 26
Francis (pope), 93
Fraud: Pacific Gas and Electric, 48
Free enterprise, 122

Galasso, Nick, 104
Gender: identity politics, 8–9. *See also* Women and girls
Geoghan, John, 91
Ghana: sexual abuse of children, 95
GI Bill, 127

Gilson, Amanda, 6
Girls. *See* Women and girls
Goddard, Henry, 22–23
Government Accountability Office (GAO): sex offenders working in schools, 97
Government Issue, 164(n13)
Great class divide, 4–5
Great Depression, 119–120, 126
Great Recession (2007–2008), 8, 111, 121–124
Greenspan, Alan, 122

Harvard College, 18
Health coverage, 61–62
Health maintenance organizations (HMOs), 60–61
Healthcare coverage: donut hole, 157(n2). *See also* Medicine
Hierarchy, ethnic groupings as, 24
Hightower, Jim, 66
Homeless individuals, 74, 105–106
Homosexuals, World War II massacre of, 26
Horace Mann School, New York, 97
How Europe Underdeveloped Africa (Rodney), 31

Identity politics, 8–9
Illness. *See* Disease
Immigrants: Melting Pot obliteration of cultures, 20–24
Imperialism: African enslavement, 17; authority of violence, 28; cheap labor and outsourcing, 29–30; decline of the empire, 35–36; environmental degradation, 30; neo-imperialism and, 36–37; New World conquerors, 14–15; normalization of violence and oppression, 25–27; racism excusing, 37; resource acquisition, 28–29; soft, 39–40; underdevelopment and exploitation, 31–32; war and massacres, 25–27
Incarceration: African Americans after Reconstruction, 19–20
Incest, 98–100
Income inequality, 104–108
India: imperial dominance, 37; monopoly control, 32
Indigenous peoples: Alaska's indigenous people, 152(n5); Anglo-Protestant holocaust against Native Americans, 12–15; extermination, 25–26; religion crowding out, 40
Indonesia, 27
Industrial recession, 119
Inequality: America's top 1 percent, 108–110; blaming the victims, 110–113; capitalist prosperity, 125–128; capitalist system increasing political inequality, 125; increasing economic inequality, 104–108; richest and poorest groups, 101–104; wealth distribution, 8, 110
Injured workers, 75
Institute on Taxation and Economic Policy, 109–110
Insurance, medical, 60–61, 68
Inuits, 152(n5)
Iran, 27
Iraq, war in, 27, 33–34
Irish immigrants, 22
Ivy League schools, 18

J.P. Morgan and Co., 21, 119, 124
Jackson, Michael, 98
Jewish communities: sexual molestation by rabbis, 94–95; stereotypes of Jewish bankers, 21–22; World War II massacre of, 26
Jobs: New Deal, 125–126
John Paul II, 85–91

Keynesianism, 128
Kozy, John, 14
Ku Klux Klan, 20

Labor: African enslavement, 16–20; cheap labor and outsourcing, 29–30; cutting medical positions, 59–61; injured workers, 75; sex offenders working in schools, 97; smart meters cutting labor costs, 54–55; strikes by medical staff, 59–61, 70; underdevelopment and exploitation, 31–32
Laissez-faire economic theory, 122, 134
Land: expropriation of native lands, 13–15
Latin America, atrocities in, 27
Latino immigrants, 23
Law, Bernard, 89–91
Lebovits, Baruch, 159(n24)
Legion of Christ, 86
Liberal media, 132
Liberation theology, 88–89, 91
Lindh, Frank, 51
Literacy: African slaves, 16
Living standards, 130–131
Living wage, 107
Lower class, 7

Maciel, Marcial, 86
Mackey, John, 66
Madison, James, 18
Madoff, Bernard, 121
Manufacturing industry: outsourcing jobs, 30
Market crisis, 118
Marx, Karl and Marxist thought, 6, 9, 118
Mass transit, 103–104
Maternity leave, 136, 165(n3)
Media: class warfare, 7; clerical abuse of children, 86; Occupy movement, 5; sexual abuse by television personalities, 98; veterans returning from the war, 127
Medical device industry, 64–65
Medicare, 61–63, 69, 131
Medicine: as market-determined, profit-driven service, 78–79; Canadian and European care, 76–78; death through medical errors, 70–72; health system mirroring class systems, 61–63; labor strikes, 59–61, 70; legal climate surrounding, 57–59; medically privileged individuals, 65–66; pharmaceutical costs, 73–74; quality and effectiveness of care, 64–65, 67–69; socialist and capitalist systems, 143–144; Swiss medicine, 75–76
Melting Pot metaphor, 11–12, 20–24
Mesirah (code of silence), 94–95
Middle class, 7–8; American prosperity in the 1950s, 128; debt, 102–103; medical care and coverage, 62; reactionary rollback of the 1970s, 132
Middle East, atrocities in, 26–27
Middle Passage, 16–17
Military and defense industries: authority of violence, 28; capitalism funding, 141; Cold War, 127–128; colonial taxes on subdued populations, 33; costs and benefits of conquest, 33–34; GIs, 164(n13); military extermination of Filipinos, 26; supremacy as goal of, 38–39; World War II production and consumption, 127
Minimum wage, 107
Moderation, ideological, 38–39
Monopoly control, 32, 122–123
Mortgage securities, 124
Mortgages, 103

Mosaic metaphor, 23–24
Munch, Peter, 21

National bank, 142
National Transportation Safety Board, 47–48
Native Americans: Alaska's indigenous people, 152(n5); Anglo-Protestant holocaust against, 12–15
NATO, 27
Neo-imperialism, 36–37
New Deal programs, 125–126
New Zealand: postal services privatization, 144
Nike, 30
Nongovernmental organizations (NGOs): democratic transformation of developing countries, 35
North Dakota, Bank of, 141–142
Northern European immigrants, 22
Nuclear power, 52

Obama administration: health care, 62–63; military expansion, 39
Objectification of the individual, 84–85
Occupy Wall Street movement, 4–5, 108, 148
Oil industry, climate change and, 140
Ontario Health Insurance Plan, 76
Organ disposal, 58
Outsourcing, 29–30
Overproduction, 118
Owning class, 7
Oxfam International report, 102–104

Pacific Gas and Electric (PG&E), 46–56
Parental leave, 136, 165(n3)
Pedophilia. *See* Sexual molestation and pedophilia
Pennsylvania State University, 97

Pentagon Keynesianism, 128
Pharmaceutical products, 64–65, 69, 73–74
Philippines: military extermination of ethnic groups, 26
Phillips, Ulrich Bonnell, 16
Pipeline explosion, 47–49
Poland: clerical abuse, 85–86
Policy goals, 40–41
Politics: action against capitalist despoilment, 148–149; economic inequality and political inequality, 125; increasing economic inequality, 104–108; political consciousness, 4
Politics (Aristotle), 23
Ponzi scheme, 121
Poorer Half, 101–108
Poverty: as way of life, 107–108; blaming the victims, 110–113; capitalism creating, 128–131; class stratification, 7–8; increasing economic inequality, 104–108; underdevelopment, 31
Powell, Lewis F. Jr., 131–132
Power: class power and wealth, 8–10
Prescription drugs: donut hole, 157(n2)
Privatization of services, 144
Professional class, minority entry into, 20
Profit maximization, 54–56
Proposition 16 (California), 54
Prostitution, 96
Publicly-owned corporations, 46–47

Quilt metaphor, 23–24
Quinn, James, 90

Rabbis: sexual molestation of children, 94–95
Race: identity politics, 8–9; racism excusing imperialism, 37; victimization of African Americans during Reconstruction, 19–20;

victimization of the working poor, 107
Rape: treatment of female slaves, 17
Recession (1900–1915), 119
Recession (2007–2008), 8, 111, 121–124
Recessions, 122–123
Reconstruction, 19–20
Red Army, 128
Refinery explosion, 52–53
Regulatory agencies: state medical boards, 65; utility accidents, 49–53, 56
Religion: Anglo-Protestant holocaust against Native Americans, 12–15; Irish immigrants, 22; pedophilia by Catholic priests, 85–93; pedophilia by Protestant clerics, 93–94; pedophilia in Mormon Boy Scout troops, 97; sexual predators as persons of trust, 84–85; soft imperialism and, 39–40
Resistance, 3
Resource acquisition, 28–32
Revolutionary insurgencies: Latin America, 23
Richards, Robert H. IV, 98
Roderick, David, 54
Rodney, Walter, 31
Rogov, Seymour, 70–72
Roosevelt, Franklin, 125–126
Roosevelt, Theodore, 119
Russia: religion as soft imperialism, 39–40

Safety concerns, 46–56
San Bruno, California, 47–52
San Onofre nuclear power plant, 52
Sandusky, Jerry, 97
Sanitation, 106
Savile, Jimmy, 98
Scahill, James, 93

Secularism as cause of clerical pedophilia, 92
Serbia, 27
Sex trafficking, 96
Sexual molestation and pedophilia: among families, 98–100; by Catholic clerics, 85–93; by celebrities and the wealthy, 98; by Orthodox rabbis, 159(n24); by Protestant clerics, 93–94; China, 96; objectification and victimization, 84–85; worldwide occurrence, 95–96
Sexual predators, 84–85
Slavery: African enslavement, 16–20; Native Americans, 13
Slovakia: health care, 77–78
Smart meters, 54–55
Social democracies, 129
Social Security, 125–126, 131
Social welfare: free market appropriation of public services, 136–138; handouts for Corporate America, 123–124; New Deal programs, 125–126; private corporations' hostilities towards, 56; rollback in the 1970s, 131–132; socialism and capitalism, 141–146; working poor, 107, 111–112
Socialism: advantages over capitalism, 141–146; publicly- and privately-owned utilities, 46–47; socialized medicine, 58, 65–66, 77–78; US view of the functionality of, 53
Soft imperialism, 39–40
Southern California Edison Co., 52
Southern Europe: early ethnic settlements, 22–23
Spanish-American War, 119
State institutions: bailing out economic failure, 120–122; using the state to protect the capitalist system, 118–120

Stereotyping: Native Americans, 14
Stock options, 63
Strikes: medical personnel, 59–61, 70
Suburbia, 128
Suicide, debt and, 106
Sutter Health, 57–59, 63
Switzerland: medical care, 75–76; minimum wage, 107

Tashi-Tsering, 95
Taxes: colonial taxes on subdued populations, 32–33; tax evasion by financial institutions, 124; tax-free income for the super rich, 109
Textile manufacturing, 32
The Utility Reform Network (TURN), 47–48
Third World: capitalism creating poverty, 129–130; underdevelopment and overexploitation, 31–32
Tibet, 40, 95
Tomasi, Silvano, 95
Transnational corporations, 29–30, 33–34
Tunisia, 4

Ukraine, 27
UN International Labor Organization, 95–96
Underclass, black, 20
Underdevelopment, exploitation and, 31–32
Unemployment: blaming the poor, 111
Uninsured citizens, 61–62, 74, 112
United Kingdom: British National Health Service, 66, 143; health care, 77; sexual molestation by BBC celebrity, 98
Utilities: privatization of, 144; socialist and capitalist systems, 143

Victimization, 84–85, 110–113

Vietnam, 26–27
Violence: as the ultimate authority, 28; normalization of violence and oppression, 25–27

Wages and salaries: doctors, 62–63; insurance and hospital executives, 63; maximizing profits at the expense of, 118–119; US working poor, 107; wage theft, 111
Wall Street: ethnic fissures in financial elites, 21–22
War on drugs, 27
War, economic stimulus following, 119–120, 126–127
Washington, George, 17
Wealth distribution: class power and wealth, 8–10; ethnic conflict resulting from, 24; slavery and class wealth, 18–19; wealth inequality, 110
White Anglo Saxon Protestants (WASPs). *See* Anglo-Protestant culture
White, Paul, 93–94
Women and girls: child brides, 96; sexual abuse of, 84–85, 95–96; treatment of female slaves, 17
Working class, 7–8
Working conditions: parental leave, 136, 165(n3)
Working poor, 107
World Economic Forum, 104–105
World War I: casualties, 26
World War II, 26, 119–120, 126
Wounded Knee, South Dakota, 13

Yale College, 18
Yugoslavia, 27

Zero sum game, 163(n31)

About the Author

Michael Parenti (PhD, Yale University) is an internationally known, award-winning author, scholar, and lecturer who addresses a wide variety of political and cultural subjects. Among his recent books are *Waiting for Yesterday: Pages from a Street Kid's Life* (2013), *The Face of Imperialism* (2011), *God and His Demons* (2010), and *Democracy for the Few*, 9th edition (2010). For further information, see his website: www.michaelparenti.org.

CPSIA information can be obtained
at www.ICGtesting.com
Printed in the USA
FSOW04n1846090817
37401FS